Exposing Yoga Myths
Be SMARTer About Your Practice
Volume 1

Exposing Yoga Myths
Be SMARTer About Your Practice
Volume 1

Kim-Lien Kendall
Melissa Gutierrez
Ariana Rabinovitch

SMARTer Bodies Press

Copyright @ 2015 Kim-Lien Kendall, Melissa Gutierrez, Ariana Rabinovitch

All rights reserved.

No part of this publication may be reproduced, distributed, or transmitted in any form or by any means, including photocopying, recording, or other electronic or mechanical methods, without the prior written permission of the publisher, except in the case of brief quotations embodied in critical reviews and certain other noncommercial uses permitted by copyright law.

Cover, layout and illustrations: Ariana Rabinovitch

The information in this book should not be used for diagnosis or treatment, or as a substitute for professional medical care. Please consult with your health care provider prior to attempting any treatment on yourself or another individual. All movement programs pose some inherent risk. As with any movement-based program, if at any time you experience discomfort, stop and consult your physician.

ISBN 978-1-329-63145-8

THANK YOU to all of our teachers. We cherish each one. There are some people who have helped us come to this particular achievement and we want to mention them.

Melissa would like to thank Eileen Muir from Karuna in Northampton, MA., Leslie Kaminoff and Amy Matthews from the Breathing Project in NYC, and every student thus far. To family and friends for their encouragement. To Elie for his never-ending love.

Ariana would like to thank all her teachers who she's learned from up close or from afar: Larissa McGoldrick, Rama Nina Patella, Jason Ray Brown, Chrissy Carter, Tzahi Moskovitz, Carrie Owerko, Dr. Kathy Dooley, Tom Myers, Gray Cook, Joseph E. Muscolino, Andrew Biel, Gil Hedley, Katy Bowman, Jill Miller, Dr. Andreo Spina, Jules Mitchell, Dr. Mark Cheng, Evan Osar, Emily Splichal, Gary Ward, Perry Nickelston, Todd Hargrove, Diane Lee, Leon Chaitow, and all the guests who have been on my Yoga & Beyond podcast from whom I've learned so much. Thank you Adam and Julia for your patience and love. To all my students and clients for going along for the ride. To friends and mentors who have inspired and guided me: Brooke Siler, Kristen Finnie Butera. To my parents, family and friends for your support even when you had no idea what I was talking about.

Kim would like to thank Amy Matthews, Leslie Kaminoff, Alison West, Nevine Michaan, Dharma Mittra, Elena Brower, Schuyler Grant, Robyn Ceballos (my first yoga class teacher) and my father (my VERY first yoga teacher) for progressing my yoga practice. Thank you to Tom Myers, Gil Hedley, Evan Osar, Emily Splichal, Ben Shear, Marcel Daane, the lovely people from Redcord Active, Bret Contreras, Tony Gentilcore and many, many more for expanding my education. Also a very big, heartfelt thank you to Sandra Jamrog. May your beautiful soul forever rest in peace, Sandy. Thank you to all of my clients and students for your loyalty and your patience. I dedicate this book to my daughter, Mya, who is my greatest teacher, always.

Our heartfelt thanks to Kris Bishop for his brilliant insight and keen advice on the production of this book.

Gratitude for our physical selves, for the information learned and for the potential within. Gratitude for the teachers and discoveries to come.

About This Book

We (Mel, Kim and Ariana) share a deep appreciation for human movement science and get frustrated when we hear false claims made in mainstream yoga and fitness media. We decided to gather some of the most prevalent myths in one place and dispel them one at a time. We thought it would be more productive than ranting about them to each other. This first volume contains general myths about yoga and yoga poses. This is a combination of expanded blog posts and new material. Because there are so many myths out there and we can't keep up, we already started working on a second volume which will contain more technical information and will debunk myths about breathing, stretching and claims about yoga cures.

What's a yoga myth you ask? Purposely misleading or unknowingly erroneous information given to the yoga-practicing public via the yoga classroom, magazines and other outlets.

Table of Contents

Introduction..................................1-4

Chapter 1:
General Yoga Practice Myths.......... 7-47

Myth 1: Yoga as we know it in the Modern West isn't real yoga, it's not pure..7

Myth 2: Yoga builds long, lean muscle.............................10

Myth 3: You should have a daily Asana practice.............................13

Myth 4: If you can't do every yoga pose then you fail to have a complete yoga practice..14

Myth 5: Yoga is the only kind of movement you need......................16

Myth 6: Yoga is a complete workout. Yoga can help you stay "fit," "get in shape," and "help you lose weight"..19

Myth 7: Yoga strengthens and stretches EVERY muscle....................21

Myth 8: Flexibility is the best thing ever. You should try to be as flexible as possible..24

Myth 9: You can't get hurt practicing yoga..25

Myth 10: Hot yoga detoxifies the body and helps you burn more calories..27

Myth 11: Always be gentle with your body. Don't push. Be super careful with yourself. Stress is bad for you..29

Myth 12: Ujjayi is the best way to breathe and you should breathe that way all the time when practicing yoga..35

Myth 13: You should always do yoga poses on the right side before the left..37

Myth 14: Squeeze your shoulder blades together and press your shoulders down your back all the time..39

Myth 15: Yoga teachers are qualified to give hands-on physical adjustments to their students, and it's ok for them to push students into the deepest expression of each pose..42

Table of Contents

Myth 16: Yoga teachers are qualified fitness professionals and you should trust everything they say..44

Myth 17: Yoga cultivates self love and positive body image.......46

Chapter 2: Myths About Poses........49-75

Myth 18: In order to use Mula Bandha in a yoga pose, you need to contract the muscles of the anus and urethra like you're holding back urine..49

Myth 19: Twists wring out the organs and detoxify the body......50

Myth 20: When you do a Twist your organs twist around your spine..53

Myth 21: Turning your head makes your Twists bigger!...............56

Myth 22: Boat Pose is a great core exercise for your abs...........59

Myth 23: Don't Use Your glutes in Bridge Pose PART 1...............61

Myth 24: Don't use your glutes in Bridge Pose PART 2................64

Myth 25: The more Chaturangas you do, the stronger your arms and shoulders will be...66

Myth 26: Your transition from Downward Dog to Plank should be seamless..68

Myth 27: Shoulderstand and Headstand are the king and queen of yoga poses...71

Myth 28: Lotus Pose is the ideal meditation seat........................74

About the Authors........................77-79

Notes & Sources........................81-88

Glossary........................89-91

Sanskrit Index........................93

Index........................95-101

Introduction

This is a guide for yoga educators and practitioners alike. Our belief in the universal value of a methodical exploration of our physical bodies is what motivates us to present this work. We love yoga and we also have a deep appreciation for science and research. We hope to demonstrate that this philosophy of subjective exploration and the endeavors of science are not mutually exclusive, nor conflicting.

We want to help yoga teachers earn a seat at the table of health professionals and raise the bar for yoga education. We encourage yoga teachers and practitioners to step outside of the yoga bubble and be willing to look to other reputable body education sources to inform (and reform) their practice and how they teach. Don't be afraid to question. Be willing to unlearn what you think you know to be true. This book incorporates the latest research and information about the human body, which is the bedrock of our work as yoga and movement educators. But tread lightly and read with a curious and critical eye.

INVESTIGATE.
DON'T REGURGITATE.

Even this academically sourced material is subject to change as new scientific discoveries are made. It's not gospel.

Belief in the inherent value of yoga postures is a slippery slope to an unjustifiable dogma. You know what we mean. We hear wanna-be axioms such as: "Twists cleanse your organs," "Being upside down increases brain activity," "Doing shoulder stand is good for the thyroid," "Belly breathing is the most beneficial way to breathe," etc. We don't agree with any of that. This disagreement is not evidence of our contrarian nature. It is evidence of the fact that we are critical thinkers who don't take information for granted without exploring it in our own bodies or doing research in the academic/scientific realm. That being said, while the 3 of us are all science-minded, we don't always agree so throughout many of the myths we share our differing opinions.

Sometimes metaphorical language can be very helpful, for instance, "breathe into your kidneys." You can't actually ever breathe into any other organ except your lungs, but directing someone's attention to their kidneys with their breath can be extremely useful. However, when making scientific assumptions we need to have our facts straight. The use of scientific jargon must be clear and definite, particularly in the efforts to legitimize the benefits of yoga.

What sets us apart:

- Like many of our beloved teachers, we do not subscribe to one system of yoga.

- We do not believe, as an absolute truth, that certain yoga poses themselves embody any inherent or immediate benefits or harm, as applied to the entire human population.

- We strive to examine and contextualize our yoga teaching in current physiology, biomechanics and neuroscience.

There are a lot of concepts and beliefs we were taught (and, admittedly, have taught) as yoga teachers that are based on conjecture or are downright false. We love to learn about the body and are always looking at how we can best help our clients and students. After all, that's what it's all about. Regurgitating myths that we were taught in teacher trainings was counterproductive. Some were beliefs that have been passed down from teacher to teacher and others were rooted in pseudoscience.

Ahimsa is a tenet of yoga (one of the 5 Yamas) – to do no harm. This also happens to be the Hippocratic oath. We'd like to take it a step further and help people live to their fullest potential by giving them accurate and truthful information.

EIGHT LIMBS OF YOGA and FIVE YAMAS

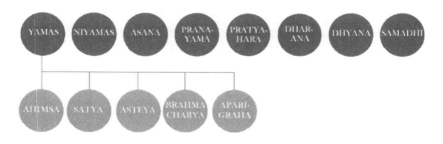

We hope to disabuse the general public of false beliefs. One being that all things "yoga" are a safe way to mindlessly approach movement while under the guidance of an often under-qualified instructor. Just like there's a lot of fitness fiction in mainstream media, there's also a lot of yoga fiction out there too. False claims based on pseudoscience permeate advertisements and yoga marketing efforts.

When we refer to yoga we are referring to "Modern" Postural Yoga. Whether utilizing the more subtle applications of yoga, meditation techniques or asanas, yoga is a tool for self-realization and self-improvement to enhance your experience in the world and in relation to others. It's a method that can and should be adapted according to the needs of the individual and the needs of the time. We often hear arguments that modern yoga isn't real yoga, or it's not pure yoga. Well, we argue that there's no such thing as an original or pure yoga. Even Krishnamacharya, who is largely responsible for spreading yoga across the continents and into the West changed his practice and changed his teaching according to the individual and according to the needs of the time. But where we draw a definitive line in this ongoing discussion is in the intention of our practice. If you are practicing because you are on a path of self-discovery then that's yoga. If you are practicing because you want to do neat tricks, bend like a Cirque du Soleil performer or want the gratification of mimicking a certain shape, then that's gymnastics. It's OK to do the latter, but that's where we draw our line.

Chapter 1

General Yoga Practice Myths

1. The Myth: Yoga as we know it in the Modern West isn't real yoga, it's not pure.

The Reality: There's no such thing as one original true form of yoga.

Yoga is a spiritual philosophy from India that predates contemporary definitions of Hinduism. The origins of this system are to this day evasive. But we do know that yoga has influenced India's religious landscape as we see it mentioned in the Bhagavad Gita and, of course, the Sutras of Patanjali[1].

Rendering of Patanjali statue

Who is Patanjali? He may have lived between 500 and 200 B.C.E. (This would be thousands of years before the formation of Christianity.) Now, talking about Patanjali like he was a real person is like talking about Jesus as if he was a real person or Buddha,

Shakespeare, King Arthur, etc. Academically speaking, the historical existence and the manner in which these individuals/traditions have manifested in our contemporary culture is constantly reevaluated and debated. (Note: We are in no way judging anyone's belief system, but are simply trying to present the academic perspective in this kind of discussion.) We'll skip that to continue giving you some background. Patanjali's writings are purported to be of Divine provenance, like many other major religious Scripture. His writings are considered to be the origins of yoga[2].

So, how did we come to associate yoga with the physical practice here in the United States? Enter Sri T. Krishnamacharya (we're sure he existed). Born in 1888, he was studying many of the spiritual systems in India, among them yoga. His career blossomed as a highly respected healer and philosopher. Many people from the West came to study with him and in 1924 the Raja of Mysore helped him to open a yoga school. The emphasis of his teachings were the physical postures that many found to be healing and enlightening[3].

Many of the poses that we're familiar with now date back to the 20th century. The stories of Krishnamacharya's education and subsequent teaching are varied and sometimes dramatic (some say he learned pranayama and three thousand postures from some dude living in a cave). Yoga was not always glorified in India. Before Krishnamacharya, yoga had a bad reputation and was used to help mentally disturbed people and societal misfits. It wasn't respected by scholars or the general public[4]. There continues to be international ambivalence concerning yoga. But Krishnamacharya broke barriers in his day and made it available to everyone: his students, his wife, his sons and daughters.

Krishnamacharya also trained three seminal teachers who further spread yoga to the west: B.K.S. Iyengar, Pattabhi Jois, and T. K. V. Desikachar[5]. All of their methods of yoga are vastly different, despite having the same source of influence. Students of these teachers then continued to spread their vision/experience of the practice and so on. One of the aspects of yoga we find so beautiful is that it is so deeply personal and so adaptable.

Krishnamacharya

Krishnamacharya himself didn't adhere to one particular yoga method. He was known to tailor the practice to the individual. When he taught the Maharaja of Mysore he taught a more vigorous practice that was more like a martial art because the royal family wanted to be strong and agile. There are also accounts of him teaching a therapeutic style of yoga that involved holding the asanas for longer.

All of these teachers most likely used the best information available to them at the time to make their teaching credible and to bring the most benefit to their students. Even though the conversation surrounding yoga is often filled with conflicting opinions one must endeavor to seek and use the best information available that will help people. We urge modern yoga teachers to participate in the forum of yoga polemics in order to ensure the integrity and positivity of what we pass on to our students.

2. The Myth: Yoga builds long, lean muscle.

The Reality: It just isn't this simple. Genetics, diet and many other factors determine how certain exercises will shape your body.

4 YOGA poses for Long Lean Legs!!!!

Ever seen a claim like this made on a popular yoga blog or magazine?

When looking at advertisements for yoga classes or when perusing through the roster of teachers at your local yoga studio, it's easy to see why one would think that the practice of yoga will yield a particular kind of body. Slender, lean yogis with visible muscular definition and bright skin, wearing scantily clad yoga apparel in pretzel-like positions with a look of serenity on their blemish-free face. Finally! The holy exercise grail of aesthetic perfection! This is certainly what a lot of these studios would want you to think in order for you to spend your money in their establishments. The marketing works perfectly for those individuals hoping to attain that type of physique, especially if they have pursued other forms of exercise that have not given them their aesthetic ideal. However, there is a harsh reality that a lot of students come to face after months of practice: It's just not that simple.

If yoga doesn't give you long, lean muscles, then why do so many yoga teachers you know have this kind of body? And why does every yoga teacher on the cover of a magazine have this kind of body? As yoga teachers who have auditioned in studio after studio, we can tell you that the unfortunate reality is effective marketing. Many studios selectively hire teachers who will bring students. Like other areas of the fitness industry, consumers are attracted to instructors who have the body that they want. How that person attained that body, however, was less likely due to their practice, but determined more by their genetics, diet, age and other lifestyle influences.

The length of muscles is determined by the bony origin and insertion points of our skeletons, which for the most part does not change. That being said, the concept of "lengthening muscles," especially from an aesthetic point of view, is a little bit absurd. Now let's address the "lean" part (or girthiness). The way that muscles grow is determined by many factors. One of the factors is tension (resistance). While it IS true that using progressive overload can build bigger (girthier) muscles WITH proper programming, this does not mean that other types of exercise can make muscles "long or lean". Aside from changing your relationship to gravity (which can change the load to a certain extent), there is a limit to the amount of resistance you can add to your workout in a yoga class. This means there is a limit to the amount of growth your muscles can have. Not only that, but given the same resistance over time, your body will adapt to that change, and not just muscularly. Your body will become more efficient neuromuscularly and you will expend less energy over time (think less calories burned) doing familiar movements with the same level of resistance. This is also why progressive overload works to promote fat loss as well, in a way that ONLY doing yoga cannot. Certain exercises can change the functional length of muscles, however, if you're just relying on yoga, expect your results to be limited.[1] For instance, strength coaches may use Romanian Deadlifts to increase the functional length of an athlete's hamstrings to prevent injury. These methods are often individualized (the weight used and amount of reps are calculated) and not something that can be achieved in a yoga class.

Another component of muscle growth is the hormonal response that causes the reaction necessary to repair muscle damage. Muscle actually grows during periods of rest that occur after a workout. How effective this process is depends on several attributes. There needs to be sufficient macronutrients present in the bloodstream (this is why diet and timing of nutrients is important)[2]. There is also an inflammatory immune response that occurs after tissue damage that is necessary for repair and ultimately growth. This complicated and not completely understood hormonal process uses IGF-1, growth hormone and testosterone along with special cells called satellite cells[3]. The amounts of these vary from person to person and a large determining factor is GENETICS. Although, certain genes express themselves at certain times because of external stimulus, ultimately it is your genetic makeup, which you have NO control over, that determines how quickly your muscles grow and how they will look when they do. Genetics also determine the constitution of connective tissue. The amounts of collagen vs. elastin determines the elasticity of connective tissue and to some degree the density of bones. These mechanical factors also will determine whether or not a person will have bulky, round muscles or "slender" muscles, despite the kinds of activity that he or she does.

Speaking of slender, when people say "long and lean muscles" they are most likely not talking about the appearance of the muscles themselves, but rather the amount of subcutaneous fat surrounding the muscles. People who show a lot of muscular definition often have low body fat percentage (which is why you can see their muscles). It is less about the actual muscles themselves. If it is fat loss you're looking for, there are a lot more effective pathways towards that goal than yoga.

So can you become long and lean doing yoga? Maybe. But the determining factor has more to do with you and less to do with yoga.

3. The Myth: You should have a daily Asana practice.

The Reality: Any movement that you do repeatedly day after day can lead to a repetitive stress injury, aka wearing your parts out.

There are messages in the mainstream yoga world that in order to be "authentic" yogis or yoga teachers it is ideal to practice yoga asana every day. Now we can debate that it's fine to have a daily yoga practice - yoga can be meditation, pranayama or acts of compassion. We're specifically talking about a daily asana practice. It's good to move and do physical things every day, but not to do the same yoga asana practice. It's not good to do any movement over and over. Yoga asanas tend to work the same muscle groups and perform the same actions in the same planes of motion. There are yoga practices that are comprised of the same repetitive poses in the same sequence, such as Bikram and Ashtanga. We strongly discourage people from doing these styles of yoga every day.

This brings to mind popular phrases such as K. Pattabhi Jois', "Practice and all is coming." We hear this used to justify interminably attempting a potentially dangerous pose until you can do it. This is why the popular social media campaign #yogaeverydamnday irked us so much. (To hear more about

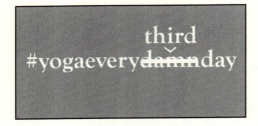

yoga every third day, listen to Yoga & Beyond episode #8 with Ariana and Jules Mitchell). Anything you do over and over again can lead to repetitive stress injuries. Chances are if you do yoga asana every day that you'll follow human nature and repeat the poses you're really good at performing. Parts of your body will wear down. Contrary to popular belief, yoga is not a complete physical practice and does not move every joint in a balanced enough way to prevent wear and tear. What you will end up doing is overstretching already elongated tissues and wearing down tissues in joints by moving them in the same directions every day. Yoga is not enough. Do other things to balance out your yoga asana practice.

4. The Myth: If you can't do every yoga pose then you fail to have a complete yoga practice.

The Reality: Not all Yoga movements or versions of poses are appropriate for all bodies.

One of the biggest misconceptions about a yoga practice is that it has to look a certain way or that you need to be able to accomplish certain movements to have a complete practice. First of all, yoga in and of itself is NOT a complete or balanced practice. There also seems to be a belief that progressions and regressions (modifications) of poses need to follow a linear pathway and in order to have an "advanced" practice, one needs to be able to follow these progressions. Not true.

If, through repeated practice, you aren't able to get your Triangle Pose (Trikonasana) to look like the teacher's, perhaps you have not failed the pose, but that version of the pose has failed you. The cues often given in yoga classes are general cues for a general body type that may not be yours. Pushing yourself into awkward positions with the mentality that you need to be able to do as the teacher is telling you can lead to injury and an overall sense of failure. Certainly not a very Yogic mindset. Given the example of Triangle Pose, it's possible that the alignment of your pelvis (perhaps it is NOT square to the side of your mat as your teacher is requesting) has less to do with your inability to externally rotate your front hip and more to do with the angle of the neck of your femur bone and how it inserts into your pelvis, which may be a different angle than your well-intentioned teacher. Continuously trying to push yourself into a position your pelvis isn't able to do can really wreck your hip joint. Or maybe binding your hands behind your back in a Revolved Side Angle Pose (Parivrtta Parsvakonasana) is just harder for you, because of your rib cage width compared to the length of your humerus (upper arm bone). Perhaps your Chair Pose (Utkatasana) can't get as deep as the next student without hyperextending in the lumbar spine, because you have longer femur bones compared to your spine length than that person. Modifying a pose, or performing it differently from the way your teacher asks, does not mean you are not a good yogi/yogini-in-the-making.

If you know that doing Chaturangas for instance, or any other asana, hurts then stop. You don't have to include it. You can still do sun salutations without hurting yourself in the process. If you want to pursue that pose, first perhaps investigate WHY this is so important to you, then go about pursuing your goal intelligently. Don't believe the hype about practicing the same way every day to get stronger. Practicing the same pattern over and over will only (maybe!) make you better at that pattern, even the pattern you're are trying to correct (i.e., won't make it better, but will make your "mistakes" more strongly ingrained). Insisting on this kind of repetition for the sake of having a "complete" practice can potentially lead to overuse injuries.

5. The Myth: Yoga is the only kind of movement you need.

The Reality: In the broad spectrum of movement, yoga makes up a small portion of what we are capable of and need for our physical well-being.

> Yoga is all you NEED.

This statement is false if we are talking about a yoga practice defined by the canon of traditional asana or the typical way yoga classes are presently being taught in the United States. Most yoga classes are taught in a very confined way, literally. Typically, students only get to explore movement that has them moving up/down and front/back (with some static rotation) confined to the space of their mat. Also, due to the lack of equipment and space, your muscles are not able to work in an even manner to balance out joint actions. Working in this way only does NOT give us the muscular adaptations needed to lift heavier things, run faster, jump higher, punch harder or throw further. That's OK, as long as students are aware of this missing movement they are skipping over in classes. That's when you can go do something else that creates that physical demand of 3-D spatial exploration like gyrotonics or dance. Or something that creates other physical demands like weight lifting or other sports.

Most of our joints move 3-dimensionally, so why would you not allow them to be used in such a way that would keep them balanced, happy and useful as you age???! Or if we are concerned with being stronger, faster, or more functional in general, why not try other forms of exercise or sports IN ADDITION TO yoga? Sticking to only one form of movement also means placing limitations on the neuromuscular patterns the body/mind will have to choose from on a daily basis. So if you also want to reduce your chances of degenerative brain diseases, like Alzheimer's, variety of movement is the spice of life. Many websites discuss how to lower one's chances of becoming a victim to this awful and tragic disease with exercise.[1] It's becoming more and more understood that placing a varied learning demand on the brain is key to keeping it healthy. Neuroplasticity is the brain's level of flexibility, which in part, has to do with how well we learn or recover from major traumas like a stroke.

Yes, we looooove Yoga and prefer its framework for slow, methodical and thoughtful physical exploration for many rehabilitation and movement re-patterning scenarios. But... some people seem to think that once you start doing yoga it's the ONLY mode of movement that you need to do. Why?

Well, one reason of many, is the widely-held belief that yoga can take care of all your physical and mental (and for some, emotional) needs. Yoga is also a seductive alternative for those who may be intimidated by other types of exercise, since it is usually deemed as "safe." People who take it for this reason falsely believe that activities like running or picking up a weight might make them herniate a disk or explode a joint. Yoga then becomes THE magical movement pill. If you do yoga you can get fit, lose weight, perform better as an athlete, reduce stress, get better sleep, become a better person, have better sex...save whales! Just kidding.

The problem is that yoga WILL NOT solve everything for you. Why? Because, no one movement modality does (and please don't even try to bring up CrossFit).

Bottom line: The more variety of movement you include in your physical demand repertoire the more movement choices available to you, which also keeps your brain healthy. Flexible body/flexible mind and vice versa.

Stop doing yoga and get a fresh perspective! - Having a long-standing yoga practice can be a wonderfully enriching part of one's life. But it can also breed a familiarity with the movements that can be stifling to one's exploration of the body. Doing something, anything completely different can benefit your practice when you return to the mat. When you give yourself a little space from yoga you can return to it with a fresh set of eyes and a new appreciation for your experience. It's good to practice with a "beginner's mind," a term used in Zen Buddhism.[2] There is no opportunity for learning if one knows it all. Give yourself the opportunity to feel something new by stepping away from the mat. Also, the better you get at other physical activities the better you might get at the more athletic aspects of your yoga practice. Learn how to do push ups well and your Chaturangas may benefit from your additional experience and strength gained off the mat. So stop confusing yoga with exercise and go do something else. Which brings us to our next myth...

6. The Myth: Yoga is a complete workout. Yoga can help you stay "fit," "get in shape," and "help you lose weight."

The Reality: Yoga does not fulfill all your workout needs (depends on how you define a workout).

Let's start by defining a workout, which can mean many things to different people. For our purposes let's say a workout is a physical activity that challenges the person with the goal of creating muscular or cardiovascular adaptation. There's nothing wrong with wanting yoga-inspired fitness. Indeed, some schools of yoga are distinctly more athletic than others. But one must be clear when using common vernacular such as "fit."

For now, let's assume we're talking about maintaining what most of society would consider a healthy weight and/or body aesthetic (we're hedging and using language very carefully here, because this subject already gets complicated and is sensitive for many, as well as subjective in nature). In order to keep up this ideal there has to be a demand placed on the physical body to exert energy and there must be challenge that a typical and long-held yoga practice most likely will not provide. There are many yoga classes that are now including jumping (plyometrics) and increasingly more physically demanding activities to satisfy those who want to keep the dream of exercise through yoga alive. Bravo! Those classes are probably great, but also cross a fine line between what is yoga **(which for us is a physical practice that allows one to learn more about the body and is less about performance)** and what is an exercise class. Again, it's OK to want yoga-inspired fitness, as long as one is cognizant of when exercise is being performed to "burn calories," "keep fit," or "lose weight." Once you've crossed that line one is no longer doing the methodical and focused practice that (in our opinion) should characterize yoga. There are many inve$ted in keeping you believing that yoga can help you lose weight. Magazines and other media outlets regularly publish articles about this daily.

Yoga can help you control and support your body weight by becoming more sensitive to the signals your body sends to you. This awareness can help you distinguish actual hunger from thirst or boredom. But it's not a enough of a cardiovascular workout for most or a strengthening program sufficient enough to produce the adaptations that most people desire. Entire muscle groups are left out and there is a limit to the amount of resistance one can add in a yoga class. External loads are essential to build strength, especially for anyone over 40 who's looking to increase their bone density!

What is and is not a workout is relative and ultimately a matter of personal opinion. We are specifically addressing overblown claims that we see repeatedly about yoga poses burning fat, boosting metabolism or causing weight loss. For someone who doesn't do any kind of movement, if yoga is all they have time for then we don't discourage them from doing it. It's better than nothing. But if the goal is purely to boost cardiovascular health, increase strength or lose weight, then other forms of exercise might be more effective in achieving those goals.

Bottom line: BEWARE the people who claim to help "raise your metabolism" doing traditional yoga. If this is the line they are trying to sell they are either blatantly lying and don't care or don't know about current exercise science.

7. The Myth: Yoga strengthens and stretches EVERY muscle in the body.

The Reality: Yoga can strengthen some muscles and can stretch some muscles.

We've read the claim that yoga strengthens and stretches every muscle in the body many times. This is something we used to believe and we still hear yoga teachers say. Much of yoga relies on personal experience and when a teacher experiences something they, naturally, want to share it with their students. However, from a biomechanical point of view it doesn't add up.

For instance, in a typical "Modern Yoga" practice we use a lot of the "pushing muscles" of the front body (think poses like Plank, Chaturanga, Downward Dog), however we don't necessarily use a lot of the pulling muscles of the back body (think muscles that would be used for pull-ups or to pull an object toward you). Similarly, there are a lot of poses which use muscles that flex the hip (think Chair Pose, Boat Pose, Downward Dog, most Warrior Poses) and not a whole lot of hip extension (except for some backbends, depending on how you do them). Due to the lack of equipment and this preference for front body muscles vs. back body muscles, it is more accurate to say that while yoga can potentially strengthen some muscles, it does not do so evenly.

Also, there is a limit to how strong muscles can get from a yoga practice. The only way to maximize strength (amount of force a muscle can apply to overcome resistance) is with progressive overload. Because a yoga practice uses only your body weight, aside from changing relationships to gravity, there will be a limit to how strong muscles can get. Furthermore, as discussed in the previous paragraph, they will not be strengthened evenly.

In order to obtain optimal joint centration (even spacing within a joint), muscles crossing over or connected directly to those joints need to be able to work synergistically. It is thought, in most schools of exercise science, that muscles can become inhibited when a muscle on the opposite side of the joint is not worked along its entire length or is held at a short length. The poses and transitions in a yoga practice don't guarantee you'll work muscles to their fullest length, especially because the planes involved in those movements don't really change (unless you purposely create 3-Dimensional movement). It is very unlikely that a regular yoga practice will stretch every muscle in your body evenly. Most practices we have seen seem to be unbalanced in their focus. For example, yogis really like stretching their hamstrings, but don't explicitly utilize hip extension to the same degree in order to stretch the hip flexors. The choices you make in your yoga practice should be dependent on who you are and what you need. Maybe you do need more hip flexion than extension! Or vice versa. But do you know why you are doing what you're doing? If not, you should explore that with a professional who can help assess your needs and create goals that will benefit you.

One of the great benefits of yoga that does distinguish it from a lot of other forms of exercise is that it has the potential to move a body through all 3 planes of motion (sagittal, frontal and transverse) in a regular practice. This potential for 3-D exploration may have contributed to the myth that yoga stretches and strengthens all your muscles. Truth be told, without equipment, it is almost impossible to accomplish this since gravity acts upon us in one direction only.

8. The Myth: Flexibility is the best thing ever. You should try to be as flexible as possible.

The Reality: Excessive flexibility can lead to instability and injury.

Flexibility is overrated. Yes, it's good to be mobile and to be able to move with ease. Perhaps it is because so many of us feel stiff and rigid, due to lack of movement, that we idealize flexibility. Maybe we have read somewhere or heard somewhere that flexibility will make us healthier and improve our lives. The problem is that we seem to live in a Type A society where everything is taken to extremes and an ideal emerges that is excluded from other factors (i.e., what do I need, what are the demands of my daily life, etc.). Flexibility is not the holy grail of fitness! Stability, strength, speed, power and cardiovascular endurance are also good movement aspirations!

Excessive flexibility is too often idealized in the yoga community and when pushed too far often leads to joint instability and injury. It's as if there is a belief that spiritual enlightenment is tied to whether or not you can get your ankle behind your neck (and if you DO believe this… sorry…). Movement variability is important for day-to-day activities. Being flexible is not going to help you carry groceries up the stairs or help you run to catch the train or defend yourself. Flexibility training or yoga are GREAT supplements to other kinds of movement, but they are certainly not ALL you need!

The kind of training you need should be based on the kind of life you have. There is this thing called the SAID principle (specific adaptation to imposed demands) which dictates that the body will adapt for that which you train it. If your daily life involves carrying a bunch of heavy stuff (new mothers who have to carry strollers up subway stairs, for instance), training SOLELY flexibility may not be the best choice. If you are on tour with Cirque du Soleil, however, and you have to hold a contorted position for a while then sure. GO FOR IT! You should ideally be training for whatever it is that you have to do. If you do yoga because you LIKE to do it, then great! Try mixing it in with some other kinds of movement.

So, what is the ideal amount of flexibility, you might ask? Again, that depends on WHAT you do. Much like the air you breathe or the food you eat, the optimal amount is what you need in the moment. If you don't need to grab your left toe with your left hand wrapped around the right side of your body to go about your day, why risk shoulder and potential knee injury? It may feel good in class, but you also have to think about your body over time and what you are demanding from it. I'm sure it's cool to touch the sole of your foot to the back of your head, but what about that deformed sacroiliac joint when you are 55? **Choose your movements and your goals wisely!**

9. The Myth: You can't get hurt practicing yoga.

The Reality: ANY physical practice can cause injury. Even sitting for long periods of time over many years can cause injury.

New students are sometimes drawn to a yoga class, because they heard or read somewhere that doing yoga is a good way to exercise without the risk of injury. Yoga classes are almost like a refuge for the injured or those just generally afraid of doing anything strenuous for fear of injury or pain. The sad truth is, NO activity you take part in has a zero percent chance of injury. In fact, you can get injured doing NOTHING. Literally just sitting there is bad for you (if you haven't read this NYT article that scared the crap out of millions of people)[1].

Speaking of New York Times articles, there was a slightly controversial one written a few years back about how yoga can wreck you[2]. Although, it can be argued that some of the research was not conducted in an unbiased manner and the author makes some claims that are a stretch of the truth (see what we did there?), it brings home a VERY important point. You can get injured in yoga just as badly as in any other physical activity (we are talking herniated disks, pinched nerves, dislocated shoulders, ACL tears, etc.). We understand how there could be confusion. How could you hurt yourself doing things so slowly like in some yoga practices? Unfortunately, you don't have to do a movement quickly to get a repetitive stress injury. Tendons, ligaments and hyaline cartilage can still be overstretched or deformed during isometric activities (holding poses for a long time, for instance). The good news here is that you do exert some level of control over this situation. Here is our advice on surviving a yoga class utilizing AWARENESS:

-LISTEN TO YOUR BODY. If something hurts, stop doing it! There is a saying "No pain, no gain," but the problem is that we tend to mistake EFFORT with PAIN. Exerting effort is hard, yes. Certainly push yourself into making a sustained effort, but not when PAIN (meaning feedback from your muscles and joints back to your brain) is involved. Learn to differentiate the two and you will be able to better reap the benefits of a yoga practice.

-DON'T assume that your teacher knows what is best for you! Your body belongs to you. It is your job to take care of it. If you are in a yoga class and the teacher is either asking you to do something that doesn't feel right or safe or is touching (aka "adjusting") you into a deeper place than you want to go, TELL HIM OR HER TO PLEASE STOP. It might be perceived as rude, but it is better than a pulled hamstring!

-DO OTHER FORMS OF MOVEMENT. Healthy, functional bodies, in our opinion, need more than what yoga alone has to offer. Plus mixing up movement, learning different patterns and introducing varied forms of stress to your body has many benefits and can actually help prevent injury! Variety is the spice of life and the foundation of a balanced body.

10. The Myth: Hot yoga detoxifies the body and helps you burn more calories.

The Reality: Hot yoga helps you lose more water. Sweating is not detoxification. We repeat. Sweating is not detoxification.

You know what doesn't rid your body of toxins? Hot yoga! You know what does detoxify your body? Your liver! Contrary to what hot yoga or juice-cleanse fanatics have to say about

> **HOT YOGA!**
>
> Sweating is one of the best ways to eliminate toxins from the body!!! The more you sweat, the more you detoxify. It's like taking a shower from the inside out!!!!!

can you sense the sarcasm?

TOXINS, we have a big, beautiful organ located in the right upper quadrant of our peritoneum that has the job of, you guessed it, ridding our bodies of toxic material (with the help of the kidneys and certain immune factors)! The great thing about this organ is that it can do all of this without the help of any weird starvation dieting or packing yourself into a 115 degree classroom with other sweaty bodies. There is VERY LITTLE real, scientific evidence that shows any benefit from practicing excessively hot yoga or doing juice cleanses for the purposes of "cleaning out" your body. That being said, there are studies concerning fasting and certain types of aggressive cancers, but for those of us who aren't suffering from a medical condition, the preventative benefits of such measures are yet to be determined[1]. But we digress… what exactly IS a toxin anyway? Kim was a biochemist and this is what she thinks about cleansing, "I have been dying to hear exact names of molecules that these yoga teachers and juicers are talking about when they say 'TOXINS', but I'm still waiting. This, my friends, is just another marketing ploy to scare you into wasting your hard-earned cash."

Now, what about hot yoga burning more calories? If you like excessive sweating and doing yoga to the point of exhaustion or to the brink of passing out in a steamy room with half naked people on slippery yoga mats then run don't walk to a hot yoga class. But don't fool yourself -- it's not a cardiovascular workout and you aren't burning more fat or calories by doing Lotus (Padmasana) in 115 degrees. You are losing water. That's all. Here's an awesome breakdown from another well written post by Michele McGinnis, "Sweat is 99% water with a dash of essential salt minerals, urea and other wastes from protein metabolism, and some trace elements like zinc. Sweat's main job is thermoregulation – to cool the body."[2] As Michele explains, sweating happens to cool us down. That's it.

While this may FEEL invigorating and FEEL like a great workout and make you FEEL clean, we mistake sweat for working harder, burning fat and calories. This feeling is what causes us to keep coming back to class. Can people lose weight from doing hot yoga every day? Sure. Especially if their level of physical activity prior to doing so involved a whole lot of nothing. Is this the most intelligent or even quickest way to lose weight and keep it off? Absolutely not.

11. The Myth: Always be gentle with your body. Don't push. Be super careful with yourself. Stress is bad for you.

The Reality: Stress (of all kinds) can actually be beneficial (and arguably necessary) for the body.

These are generally good rules to listen to when challenging yourself physically and trying to avoid injury, especially when learning a new activity. But if one uses this kind of thinking to dictate how she should treat the body in all situations it can actually be counterproductive to health and well being. Stress (of all kinds) can actually be beneficial (and arguably necessary) for the body. See one of our favorite TED talks about this from Kelly McGonigal[1].

Now, let's talk about gravity. Throughout the course of our entire lives as mobile human beings we actively engage with the oppressive and compressive forces of gravity (and other natural forces). For everyday activities from locomotion, to breathing we must combat and even use those gravitational forces to assist us in living healthy lives. Make no mistake. It is by intelligently dealing with stressful elements that we can strengthen all aspects of our physical bodies (as well as our mental and emotional bodies). Knowing when to back off is a necessary skill, but don't think you need to always use kid-gloves.

Here are examples of this behavior that we find significantly detrimental:

- It is assumed that you need more props in your yoga practice as you age. That's a bit presumptuous. Age, in and of itself, is not always a direct indicator of "level of ability" in a yoga class. Yoga Journal recently had an entire spread about how to keep your yoga practice safe as you age and YJ suggested adding more props[2]. Wouldn't one think that as we age it is more important to be confident in our bodies, knowing how to securely traverse space around us? Stability is key for all of us. In particular, stability can save us from a nasty fall, which can be harder to recover from as we age (falls are one of the determining factors of death in people over 65. Look at the stats[3]). If the idea is to use yoga to keep bones strong and improve stability, then let's create a practice that allows people of all ages to challenge themselves and encourage them (safely) to better manage themselves and their bodies without the fear of, "If I don't have a wall or a prop I can't do this, because I'm older." Perhaps props will be needed (as with anyone of any age) if the practice is new, but a worthy eventual goal is to be able to manage your body without assistance, **no matter what your age.**

- "Be careful with your back." We hear from clients ALL THE TIME how they are careful performing movements that can "hurt their backs," even though they do not currently experience back pain. This often includes twisting (trunk rotation) and extension in the lower back. With the exception of people who actually do have back pain and/or were diagnosed with a condition (which is a VERY GOOD reason to actually be careful with your back), we find that a lot of people seem to have rumor-driven back anxiety. What's interesting with this kind of spinal-anxiety is that if you pursue a line of questioning to zero in on his or her concerns, there is no real reason. We hear: "I've heard that too much lumbar curve isn't good"; "I don't want to twist and possibly create a bulging disc"; "Sometimes my back is sensitive, so I treat it tenderly." It seems the fear of future back pain can create a hyper-awareness of any kind of sensation, painful or not. This lack of discrimination leads to making choices about movement that are misinformed and can lead to neurotic, self-imposed limitations. Try googling about back pain and getting out of bed (then try googling what Dr. Sarno[4] has to say about bulging discs and back pain.). There are many, many articles advising people about how to get out of bed! Some of these articles are written by doctors and physical therapists who would warn you to avoid twisting as much as possible when getting up. Or even doing stretches before getting up. Seriously... It's not wrong to take special care of yourself, especially if you have just suffered an acute injury. But wouldn't it be more helpful to assist a person to finding mobility that feels good and healthy that removes anxiety over the simplest of acts? If you're obsessing about how to properly get out of bed to avoid injury, then you should be equally as concerned with walking, carrying anything, eating, sneezing or going to the bathroom (which can actually cause a lot of internal pressure changes on the spine.) Unless there are specific structural issues, getting out of bed, bending over to pick up your child or doing many other everyday tasks should be a gift that you should be able to take for granted. Check out this video[5] that we send to clients who are dealing with a fear of back pain from Peter O'Sullivan.

- "I don't EVER jump or run, because it stresses my joints unnecessarily." Your body and joints are built to withstand a good amount of impact and stress in moderation. But as with everything it is about how you perform any activity (how much load, how frequently and more importantly how you are using your body to do it). Running and jumping are activities that have allowed our species to survive (Oh no, I can't get away from this hungry lion for fear that I might hurt my joints... can you imagine?). The structure of our feet and legs tells the story of our running and jumping ancestry (yes, we know short vs long distance running is still being debated BUT, it can be agreed that we did run at one point or at least we sprinted!). We agree that running and jumping with improper shoes on flat, hard or paved surfaces with feet that no longer fully-function because of being used to hard-soled shoes will inevitably cause problems. However, there are plenty of ways to get around this and plenty of people who can help train you to do these things properly. We are not saying that everyone has to run and jump. If you don't want to, then don't do it (hope you never get chased by a lion...). But don't stop yourself because you are afraid that those things are bad for you. What happens when you trip and fall? What if that fall is the first real hard impact your body has to deal with? Chances are, since it's not used to handling those kind of intense physical vectors of force that travel through the body upon impact, it may not cope well (and we are not even getting into what the brain does, reflexes, etc). People who practice these actions on the regular have better chances of falling and getting back up without much drama (obviously too much practice is not good either). Also, jumping is great for moving lymph in the body and keeping bones healthy. So, don't fear impact. Engage with it intelligently and use it to your benefit.

- "Organs are delicate"... Some people are afraid to get in touch with their organs figuratively and literally. For some it can be just plain gross, which is understandable, but is an attitude that should be changed. Bodies are visceral experiences (puns!) and allowing yourself to be familiar with what's going on inside of yourself can bring up emotions, but the process is completely worth it. Your body is your house and it is YOUR responsibility to take care of it. Get to know what is going on. Some people may advocate that we should use extreme caution when dealing with organs and that too much movement or touch can be hazardous to their well being. Do understand that we REGULARLY put stress on our organs already by being alive (have you ever breathed or eaten anything or went to the bathroom?). We sometimes bump into people or walls and this jostles our insides. Some of us are stomach sleepers with no fear of rupturing intestines. You might be a little sore upon waking up, but everything remains intact. Reject the idea that your insides are delicate. If they were delicate, we would probably not have evolved skeletally with a big GAPING HOLE exposing our most delicate features (of course this leaves organs somewhat vulnerable to knife fights, Muay Thai competitions and shark attacks. But we would be so much heavier if we had ribs all over our bellies and that would definitely change breathing). Your organs can provide immense support for the arrangement of the musculoskeletal system. Remember our post about organs supporting you?[5] If you could watch a video of what was going on inside your body even while you are just sitting on the couch watching the Housewives of Beverly Hills (one of Mel's favorites!), you would be amazed at how much movement you would observe (you might even stop watching Bravo, because your organs are way more interesting!). Embrace their strength and rest assured that so much of your personal durability is because of your organs' strength.

There are so many ways in which we try to control our life experiences in order to avoid pain and create safety. We can create this control through fear or anxiety and limit the physical experiences in our bodies to ensure that we are not stressed. The problem with this is 2-fold.

a) You will inevitably have your safety bubble popped, because we live in a world full of stressors. Relationships, environment, illness…You will be under prepared for handling them well when confronted.

b) This fearful behavior will negatively color much of your attitudes towards movement. You will limit and inhibit yourself, which can lead to many physical issues. The body is a machine that needs movement (challenging movement) to remain healthy and capable. You start to communicate fear to the body and allow that to manifest as physical anxiety and you've created a perfect storm for all the problems you'd like to avoid. In other words, don't wait until you are being chased by a lion to learn how to move… you'll get eaten.

Remedy the fears. Get rational. Educate yourself. Train so that you can be functional in an often dysfunctional world. Know what your body truly is and isn't capable of and then you can start making the kind of decisions that will keep you healthy and happy.

12. The Myth: Ujjayi is the best way to breathe and you should breathe that way all the time when practicing yoga.

The Reality: Ujjayi is A way to breathe that requires a tensing of muscles in the throat which constricts the trachea or at the very least puts pressure on it. It's not necessarily a great way to breathe when you're trying to move around.

It has been said that Ujjayi breathing slows down the breath, extending the inhalation which allows more oxygen to enter the bloodstream. It's also been claimed that extending the exhalation expels more toxins.

In reality, lengthening the duration of the inhale does not increase oxygen intake. The amount of oxygen that enters the bloodstream depends on many other biochemical factors. Furthermore, carbon dioxide is expelled on the exhale not toxins.

Here's when we might suggest Ujjayi to a student - they're having trouble focusing on their breath. It's just so far out of their awareness that they have no idea what they're supposed to do when told to "be aware of the breath." Ujjayi can be useful in this instance, because they will be able to hear the breath. It becomes an auditory stimulus for them and perhaps that will help them notice it more.

Here's when we tell students to stop doing Ujjayi completely - when it's clear that they're doing it repeatedly in an unconscious way. They're not even aware that they do it all the time and have a hard time stopping. Part of yoga is to become aware of habits and not get tied to them. To breathe in Ujjayi one constricts the throat and the glottis. This restricts and controls the flow of air in and out of the trachea. It also creates tension in the throat and neck. In our opinion this is not an inherently beneficial way to breathe, especially when moving. The flow of air should be unfettered. Neck, jaw and throat tension should be minimized.

Many of the pranayama practices are refined and controlled breathing practices. This kind of sophisticated breath manipulation can be useful. But there is danger in adopting a pattern of having to be in a constant state of control. This may be excitatory to your nervous system as opposed to relaxing. Ask yourself if you're able to truly let go during a yoga or meditation practice. Must you always consciously manipulate your breath to feel safe? Can you relax and trust the body's autonomic functions to make breathing happen without you having to dictate? These are valuable questions to explore. There is just as much value in letting go as there is in performing conscious breathing patterns.

13. The Myth: You should always do yoga poses on the right side before the left.

The Reality: There is no scientific justification for this theory.

According to some yoga methods, the right side is the more active "sun" side and the left is the calmer "moon" side. It's often said at the end of a yoga class after Savasana to lie on the right side to keep the more active side subdued before coming up to sit. It's also often suggested to do the right side before the left in every pose and to twist to the right prior to twisting to the left.

Systems of medicine that are explicitly based on the use of energy flowing through the body (i.e., acupuncture, Ayurveda, etc.) may be more supportive of this theory. Some people use yoga in this way. We don't (but do support other beneficial aspects of yoga), so we're going to keep our explanation in the context of the physiology we utilize in SMARTer Yoga™[1] and Foundations of Movement[2]. This is part of the difficulty of culturally appropriating spiritual/esoteric practices like yoga and trying to apply them to a different demographic.

In regards to twists specifically: One justification we've heard about twisting to the right first is that the colon is structured from right to left and moves its contents along this pathway. The enteric nervous system is very sensitive and responsive to touch. So, if you were doing visceral massage we would go with what's typically been taught and massage right to left in order to help facilitate the movement described above. But, twists are not massage and do not provide the direct pressure that a massage would since the whole torso is twisting AS A WHOLE. While it may FEEL like we are twisting around our spines and creating a LOT of movement, in reality this just isn't the case.

Let's put "yoga advice" in the context of daily living. If the advice you were given is true then you should be worried of ever having to spontaneously rotate your trunk to the left. This happens countless times in a day. Imagine having dropped something on the left and you pick it up with your right hand. Does that mean you now have to develop an OCD-like ritual to compensate for twisting "against your colon?" Doesn't seem functional for easy living.

Now within the context of Neuroscience: The human brain is bilaterally organized, meaning we have a right and left hemisphere that is connected by the corpus callosum. When these two halves of the brain control our limbs they do so contralaterally. Left brain is in charge of the right side of the body and right brain is in charge of left side of the body. Guaranteed, if you google, "trunk rotation and bilateral organization of the brain," you will find a plethora of scientific and movement oriented literature that suggests crossing our midlines is necessary for optimal brain function. We doubt that our brains and bodies would be constructed in this way if we had to be so careful about, what is to most of us, casual and unconscious movement. If, having been born structurally normal, we shouldn't have to care about which direction and order we rotate our trunks.

It doesn't make evolutionary sense and it flies in the face of the principle of homeostasis.

14. The Myth: Squeeze your shoulder blades together and press your shoulders down your back all the time.

The Reality: Doing this all the time is bad for your shoulders and back and can create excessive muscular tension.

There's nothing wrong with learning to roll your shoulders away from your neck and ears, especially if you have a habit of keeping tension there (after long days at work for instance) and more so if you cannot tell the difference between when your shoulder blades are up and when they are down. It's also important to know the difference between shoulder blade movement, spinal movement and arm movement. But there's no benefit to constantly shoving your shoulders down your back ALL the time and in EVERY yoga pose. Let's use two main points to illustrate.

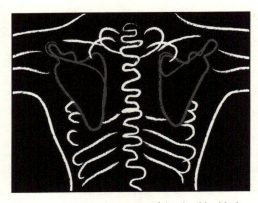

Artsy anatomical representation of the shoulder blades on the back

Moving the shoulders down your back does not always improve posture. Most of the time, posture has more to do with your spinal alignment than anything else. If your spinal alignment is off, this affects your posture, but for most people this seems to be the most visible in the shape of the shoulders. The shoulder blades (scapulae) are not directly attached to your spine, they are attached to the collarbones and upper arm bones only. Pulling the scapulae down the back or squeezing them toward each other may give you the feeling of better posture simply because you are stretching certain muscles that may be shortened throughout the day, but the reality is that moving your shoulder blades by themselves does not move the spine or make you sit up straighter. Should you learn to relax the shoulders down...YES! One way to do so is by visualizing your lungs and breathing so that you can create space within the rib cage, upon which you can gently rest the shoulder blades. Learning to do this will give the shoulders the supportive feedback they need in order to relax and release any tension they may be holding.

Pulling your shoulders down does not necessarily help you relax. If you do it all day long, it will LIMIT your ability to breathe! Holding yourself in this restrictive position ties up muscles that would be normally used for breathing into the upper portions of your lungs and will not allow for the full potential of an inhalation. In a forward bend you'll often hear the teacher say to move your shoulders down your back. This in itself is not a bad tip, especially if one is working toward a particular experience. But if the goal is to relax, it is also just as important to allow the shoulders to fall forward and yield to gravity, which is the hallmark of being relaxed.

Another example is when you are told to pull your shoulder blades down when your arms are lifted above your head. Not only does this interfere with proper breathing patterns, but it is DETRIMENTAL to shoulder function. There is this thing called the scapulohumeral rhythm[1] that essentially dictates where your shoulder blades need to be given particular angles of your arm bone from your body (It is far more complicated than that, but this will do for now.). When your arms are over your head, your shoulder blades should be UPWARDLY ROTATED and the muscles involved in this (the serratus anterior, etc.) need to be fully engaged so that if you are to change your relationship to gravity and bear weight (as in Downward Dog or Handstand) you won't injure yourself. Screwing up your scapulohumeral rhythm with intentionally poor patterning like restrictive scapular movement can really screw up your shoulder and cause rotator cuff tears.

So, the next time you find your shoulders up to your ears and you want to relax them, do some shoulders rolls to loosen up the muscles. Or try breathing into your "upper lungs" and letting your blades rest and yield to gravity. Do not pinch them in the back or try to keep shoving them down your back. Breathe, feel the lungs fully inflate and move the rib cage. Practice until you feel the shoulders surrender and float up and down (passively) with each breath. If you do intend to work on your posture (for whatever reason), start with the hips and/or spine and see how this affects your shoulders and neck (we build our stance from the bottom up, n'est-ce pas?).

15. The Myth: Yoga teachers are qualified to give hands-on physical adjustments to their students, and it's ok for them to push students into the deepest expression of each pose.

The Reality: Not so fast. We argue that unless a teacher is also a qualified physical or manual therapist (whose certification requirements are way more rigorous than a yoga teacher's) he/she should not adjust his/her students.

Yoga teachers are taught many hands-on adjustments, some more intrusive than others. In some states personal trainers aren't allowed to touch their clients. We err on the side of caution and prefer a light touch to serve as guidance (external cuing) rather than pushing people into correct positions, which is what we have seen and experienced a LOT of teachers do. Most of us are taught to do this.

Just because a yoga teacher has taken one or two teacher trainings, doesn't mean they have the skill required or anatomical knowledge to adjust students safely. Did you know that massage therapists have to take approximately 1-2 thousand hours of course study and then apply for a license before they are allowed to touch their patients? And yet, in yoga teacher trainings we are taught many hands-on adjustments while students are in considerably vulnerable positions. Many of these adjustments are intended to bring the student "deeper" into the stretch. Maybe that deeper stretch isn't right for that student's body. Maybe their body just isn't ready for it. It may be best to err on the side of caution and a.) ask before you adjust, b.) try to get them to find it themselves or c.) don't touch.

We've seen photos and videos of "gurus" and established well-known yoga teachers giving adjustments that look downright violating and violent. We've seen teachers stand on a student's back to encourage deeper forward bends, standing on thigh bones to encourage more external rotation at the hip, and worse. We've also experienced these pushy adjustments from both experienced and inexperienced teachers in group classes. Using brute force to push the body into a preconceived idea of how the pose should look is not OK. **If you're a teacher, don't do this to your students. If you're a student, don't let the teacher do it to you.** Simple as that.

16. The Myth: Yoga teachers are qualified fitness professionals and you should trust everything they say.

The Reality: The yoga world is riddled with much ambiguity concerning certifications.

To be a personal trainer, in most gyms, you need to pass an examination by a nationally recognized organization in order to receive a certification (which still means VERY little, but at least it's something). To be a massage therapist, depending on the certifying organization, you need to put in THOUSANDS of hours and apply for a license. To be a yoga teacher... you pretty much just have to tell people you teach yoga and hopefully have personal liability insurance. SOME gyms and most yoga studios will require that you have taken at least a 200-hour training (which can be done in as little as 6 weeks) and are registered with Yoga Alliance (an overseeing body that teachers pay a small fee to and, to which, teacher trainings pay a bigger fee). Being registered with Yoga Alliance is a suggestion, but not a requirement. For example, Mel and Kim are not registered, but Ariana used to be. We've based the decision not to register on personal opinions. As you can see, not being registered with Yoga Alliance does NOT make someone an unqualified teacher.

Therein lies a potential problem. There really is NO standard as far as teacher qualifications go. Not only that, but being a yoga teacher is a very attractive part-time gig since the return on investment can be huge. One can spend several hundred on a 200-hour training, get a couple of private clients and start making $200 a pop to go to someone's house and teach them a simple yoga sequence! No one is the wiser! So what's the problem?

The problem is that we end up with a whole bunch of under-qualified individuals teaching movement and adjusting eager students. A lot of these teachers have NO prior background in anatomy or human movement studies and took a 200-hour training with VERY LIMITED time spent on anatomy or kinesiology. To add another layer of potential catastrophe, most teachers are encouraged to do manual adjustments. Recipe = disaster.

We aren't trying to discourage anyone from taking yoga classes (we teach yoga, duh!), but we are suggesting that perhaps you exercise some critical thinking. There are some absolutely brilliant and completely qualified yoga teachers out there, but there are also some who … you probably shouldn't be taking any advice from. Like any advice about anything. One way to distinguish a qualified teacher from an unqualified teacher is to ask about their backgrounds. Ask what their continuing education has been? How many private clients do they have? If you are seeking help with a specific issue ask them about that issue and see how they answer ("I have spinal stenosis, what do you recommend?" "Well let's do Cobra Pose to strengthen your back," is not an ideal answer. They should be asking you specific questions about your condition. This is for the teacher's safety as much as yours.)

Don't be afraid to investigate your teacher's background. Be aware and practice safely!

17. The Myth: Yoga cultivates self-love and positive body image.

The Reality: Yoga has the potential to promote positive body image, but it's not removed from the rest of the fitness industry. Competition among students, body image issues and eating disorders are just as prevalent here as they are anywhere else.

As stated in previous myths, one of the reasons that people are drawn to yoga is the incorrect assumption that doing yoga will give them a body like their yoga teacher (please read Myth #2). A lot of women, unfortunately, are still under the impression that strength training will make them bulky (no no no NO!) and prefer to take up activities like yoga and pilates in an attempt to live out their fantasies of being thin. Now imagine a room full of people like this who are encouraging each other to do juice cleanses and adopt a vegan diet. Sounds healthy, right? This could actually be a potentially hazardous environment. Individuals with serious body dysmorphia and eating disorders may be propagating unhealthy and dangerous habits by coming to yoga classes that make claims about "healthy living" couched in pop-science or pseudoscientific language. In the industry of self-love and self-acceptance low-carb diets, chronic juicing/cleansing and obsessive calorie counting are examples of pathological and neurotic behavior that goes unchecked, because the context in which it occurs is a socially desirable one.

We have heard terrible, TERRIBLE things from our students like "I would be able to do this bind in Revolved Triangle (Parivrtta Trikonasana) if my waist was just a little smaller". Wait…you want to change the shape of your body to be able to touch your hands behind your back while you are twisted around awkwardly?! And what exactly would this accomplish? If you feel guilt or shame to the point that you would try to lose body fat, so that you can do a "picture perfect" pose, this is NOT yoga! That is body contortion and probably some form of body dysmorphia.

In NYC, hot yoga, "power" yoga or vinyasa classes, seem to attract Type A personalities. As such, you might find a room full of scantily clad, green-juice drinking yogis all trying to competitively out-pose each other. This is unfortunately NOT the kind of environment people with any level of body insecurity (read: almost EVERYONE) can thrive in. If this is the kind of thing you are into, feel free and pose away. However, if you are coming to the practice hoping to find a refuge where you can learn to become confident and build a healthy relationship with your body, know what to expect and please choose your classes wisely!

Bottom line: The practice should release you from your ego. Your ego should not be dictating the practice.

Chapter 2

Myths About Poses

18. The Myth: In order to use Mula Bandha in a yoga pose, you need to contract the muscles of the anus and urethra like you're holding back urine.

The Reality: Mula Bandha is, perhaps, more accurately, a contraction of muscles of the pelvic floor.

Mula bandha according to Iyengar is a posture where the muscles from the anus to the navel are contracted, lifted up and towards the spine.[1] It seems that Iyengar is using a language that attempts to describe an experience, but unfortunately his anatomical reference is incorrect. A properly executed Mula Bandha may feel the way Iyengar describes it (and may even energetically correspond to the entire area he refers to), but what you are really engaging is your pelvic floor. This is an important distinction to make since YOUR PELVIC FLOOR IS NOT RESPONSIBLE FOR STOPPING THE FLOW OF URINE! It is your urethral sphincter and your external anal sphincter that are responsible for controlling the stream of urine or feces. Therefore, pretending to hold the stream (like we've heard cued in classes) in an attempt to access your entire pelvic floor DOES NOT NECESSARILY WORK.

Your pelvic floor, or pelvic diaphragm, is a group of muscles that includes the 3 muscles of your levator ani (pubococcygeus, puborectalis, and iliococcygeus) and your coccygeus muscle[2]. Some refer to the entire pelvic floor by referencing only one of the muscles, abbreviated as the PC. Both men and women have these muscles, and just like any other skeletal muscle, they need to be conditioned for both sexes. Unconditioned pelvic floor muscles can lead to prolapsed organs, incontinence, more subtle breathing issues or the inability to properly create intra-abdominal pressure for core work or problems lifting things in general.

A well conditioned pelvic floor will be helpful for birth labor, core strength and organ health. Regardless of the cultural context, this muscular work is important and relevant to every human being. That being said, we shouldn't walk around contracting our pelvic floor muscles all the time. Just like any other muscle in the body, these should be able to contract, stretch and have a healthy normal resting tone.

Look in the sources/notes section for a link to bonus pelvic floor exercises.[3]

19. The Myth: Twists wring out the organs and detoxify the body.

The Reality: Your organs are protected by your skeletal structure, layers of muscle, fat and connective tissue. You can move them around a bit depending on your position but you can't wring them

out, nor would you WANT to.

You know what doesn't rid your body of toxins? Twists! You know what does detoxify your body? Your liver! (And your kidneys, lungs, lymph...)

We've heard many a yoga teacher say that twists "wring out the organs." Some even go as far as to say they should be done as part of cleanses and can rid the organs of toxins, and that when you release from the twist, your organs are "filling with fresh blood."

Twists can perhaps compress the organs a bit, but they don't wring them out. So, what are twists good for? Twists can be good for the spine. When you rotate the spine it compresses the discs between the spinal joints and then when you return to a "neutral spine" the discs come back to the uncompressed state. This kind of movement lubricates the joints and helps to maintain the plumpness of the discs so they don't deteriorate or dry out from lack of use. It's also good to move the muscles and fascia in your torso around in that way, but it's not about wringing out organs like a towel to rid the body of toxins.

Our abdominal organs (with the exception of your kidneys and, arguably, part of your spleen and this probably changes from person-to-person) are encased in a sac called your peritoneum,[1] which is tethered loosely in place by ligaments. Some of these organs are vacuous (like the stomach and intestines) and some are not (like the liver). When you compress the outside of the peritoneum, the organs will glide around and compress a little. This external movement helps to facilitate an internal movement, which can be helpful in many ways. Since organs, like so many parts of the body, benefit and function best when moved, twisting can be super helpful for digestion since the contraction of our intestines (peristalsis) is stimulated by touch. We wrote this post[2] awhile back about breathing and digestion, and the same principles apply here. It's safe to say that the body does not function optimally in a stagnant state. So twist and do so knowing that you are helping to create movement in your internal organs, but in NO WAY are they "wrung out." That's not possible and if that happens to you or inside of you please go to a hospital, because you are going to die.

Also, do the organs fill with fresh blood after trunk rotation? No, they are CONSTANTLY filled with "fresh" (We're assuming this means oxygenated) blood, because we have these vessels called ARTERIES whose job is to deliver this type of blood constantly from birth to death. If this didn't happen, our organs would die and so would we. And what exactly do they mean by removing "toxins?" This is a much debated topic in body science, but if they mean that twisting movements can assist in a metabolic process even on the cellular level or by moving fluids or stimulating the lymphatic system then maybe. But only because ALL movement helps to facilitate metabolic processes on just about all levels.

Now, none of the above means that you can't enjoy metaphor and imagery like, "imagine twisting and creating a spiral staircase of your organs." That's OK if that's how it FEELS to you. It's OK if you FEEL like your organs are in a Coney Island Carnival Carousel accompanied by the NYC mermaids[3]. This is the beauty of a practice like yoga where one can explore and connect to the uncharted territory of the internal landscape. You can FEEL many things that not everybody else does and that experience is valid (Kim hates the "staircase of organs." Mel and Ariana don't mind it. And yet, we coexist.). But understanding the anatomical reality is a good place to start when contextualizing, making sense of and sharing that experience with others.

As stated above, yes, movement is GOOD for the body. Therefore, twisting can be really good for improving digestion and perhaps for relieving acute constipation, gas and other general indigestion symptoms (notice we didn't say CURE). But it should be noted that not everyone's guts or enteric nervous system enjoys being so stimulated. Again, you will find exceptions to every rule. So as long as twisting doesn't aggravate an already agitated system then feel free to enjoy. Go forth and twist as much as you want, safely of course (respecting the limitations of your body)! Because, now that you know what's really going on in the body, you have better chances of performing twists with awareness, which opens the door to the REAL possibilities and benefits.

20. The Myth: When you do a twist your organs twist around your spine.

The Reality: Your organs don't twist around your spine. The peritoneum is ALWAYS in FRONT of the spine...with no exception.

For context, imagine lying on the floor with your knees twisting to one side and your head twisting to the other. You might feel or (if you were in class) be directed to allow "the internal organs to twist around your spine," BUT they don't.

The peritoneum (the sack of connective tissue that contains most of the internal organs) is ALWAYS in FRONT of the spine…with no exception. In a different relationship to gravity, such as a seated twist, you may FEEL as if the organs are moving around the spine, especially if you turn your head to the opposite direction than your knees. Doing so can enhance sensations, because you're playing with proprioception, nervous system functions, and if the muscles on the front of the body are tight then you are feeling them stretch. Don't confuse feeling muscles stretch, connective tissue movement and tracking the subtle spinal sensations for exaggerated organ movement.

You might be wondering if it's even possible to feel your organs. Well, this a good time to talk about interoception. We get information from inside ourselves all the time. Yes, most of us know about proprioception and how that process allows us to properly orient our physical selves in our external environment. Having a consistent yoga, dance or other conscious movement practice can help increase our abilities to propriocept keenly resulting in (possibly) better balance, confidence in ourselves and refined motor skills. But our brains are also constantly receiving information from the internal landscape of our physical selves. Your organs speak to you via interoception. That pressure you feel when you have to pee? That's your bladder signaling, "Hey, now's a good time to get emptied." The gnawing hunger that gets more intense with time? That's your tummy telling you that calorie intake is necessary to keep you going.

You may not be as comfortable or accustomed to paying conscious attention to your organs the way you do your muscles and bones. But if wish to live a life of overall health and well being then you better start making the time and space to explore yourself on a more profound level. This can happen during meditation in which you practice detaching from all the outside stimuli (processing external stimuli is called exteroception) while honing in on what you are feeling deep within. The other side of this coin is that you can dampen those signals and become deaf to your body's internal communication by ignoring it. Simple as that. If you insist on ignoring your hunger, thirst, bathroom and other primal needs you force your body to start communicating in "louder" less pleasant ways. Ever waited too long to eat, because you were busy working or playing or whatever? Bet you became a pretty nasty person (hangry) or you get emotional or you feel sick or you want to faint…we've made our point. Dulling your interoceptive capabilities also makes you easily fooled into believing something is happening to you in yoga when it isn't, like the organs wrapping around your spine thing. **(BTW, ignoring your physical needs is a lot like ignoring your emotional needs. Doing so usually garners negative results. This is a clear example of how a successful yoga practice lets you FEEL on many levels).**

Your organs are a part of your daily experience whether or not you choose to pay attention to them. But if you do, you'll be better equipped to make beneficial decisions about the food you eat, what you drink, what kind of exercise you need, how much rest you should get and where you tend to feel emotions and how to better process them. Once those signals become clear to you, then perhaps you can start to differentiate whether your liver needs attention or your back hurts because your muscles are sore or maybe your kidneys need a break from the hyper-adrenalized existence you impose on them. **GET IT YET?!** Listen to what's going on inside and be the leader of your own health and balanced living revolution.

21. The Myth: Turning your head makes your twist bigger!

The Reality: Turning the head may or may not increase the twist throughout the spine as much as one feels. You might be surprised how this head turning action can fool you into skipping over movement in the thoracic spine or other places.

Frequently in yoga classes we are directed to turn the head in the opposite direction of the knees to "increase the twist." But it may be more important to track the subtle sensations and know from where we are twisting than be concerned about how far we can go. Sometimes turning the head can make us lose track of those sensations. Yoga provides an opportunity for self-exploration that can be more valuable than shape making. So let's explore what's happening and what contributes to what we feel.

Turning your head, with the eyes closed, can enhance sensations coming from the muscles. Turning the head may or may not increase the twist throughout the spine as much as one feels. Muscles and fascia connect the skull to the spine and front of the ribs. When one rotates the head these structures may move as well. Depending on your flexibility in these muscles and connective tissue, this movement can feel small or large. Also, if your eyes are open visual stimulus may override what you've been feeling and your gaze may lead you to believe that your head and other parts of your body may be facing that same direction. You may feel sensations from your sensory organs that you're turning to a satisfactory degree to yourself or your teacher, but this still does not mean that you are increasing the distribution of the twist "evenly" throughout the entire spine. How well you propriocept (the nervous system function that gives us the ability to sense our bodies from within) is what can trick you into believing that turning your head is actually increasing your twist in a way that is more significant than what is actually happening. You might be surprised how this head turning action can fool you into skipping over movement in the thoracic spine or other places.

Even now while sitting at your desk, if you twisted to one side and used your head with the eyes closed you might be very surprised to see where the rest of your body is in space if you lined up your nose with your sternum and then opened the eyes. This information isn't here to suggest that you need to exploit more movement in the spine to go farther. The structures that make up the spine influence the varying degrees of flexibility and movement available along it. This varies from person to person.

The facet joints, the joints between the vertebrae, are shaped and oriented differently in each section of the spine. In the cervical spine the shape of the facets allows for more rotation, in the thoracic spine the facets allow for more lateral flexion, and in the lumbar spine the facets allow for more flexion and extension. Because we tend to exploit the rotation

Degrees of Freedom (Movement) of the Spine

	FLEXION	EXTENSION	ROTATION	LATERAL FLEXION
CERVICAL	70-90	70	90	20-45
THORACIC	20-40	15-30	5-20	25-30
LUMBAR	40-60	20-35	3-18	15-20

note: opinions and sources differ on the degrees of movement of the spine [1]

available to us in the cervical spine, combined with the visual stimulus of our gaze we may be fooled into feeling that we are in a "full twist" when we are actually just compensating for lack of movement or awareness in another segment.

You may be using your head to overcompensate for movement you may not have available in the thoracic or lumbar spine. Compensating in this way may not be great for your cervical spine. Or, in your rush to meet your end goal, you may be skipping over movement you didn't realize you had in other places that would assist you in performing your twist. This same process of compensation can be applied to backbends. One thinks they are "evenly" distributing extension when in reality there's a lack of awareness of how the spinal structures are really arranged. Either way, in the name of doing yoga to gain more awareness and refine the connection you have to your body this is evidence that you need to be paying closer attention.

Try the seated twist again, but this time try to track the movement of it throughout your spine starting at the bottom (there may even be slight movement of the sacrum, but whether there should be and how much is another discussion. If you have questions about this contact us). As you "twist" your way up see if there are places in the spine you may not be aware of (consciousness). If so, go back, slow down and then proceed. This time, can you keep track of all that movement in all those places and not lose your sense of it when you turn the head? If you kept track: Bravo! You're gaining new ground in creating flexibility, not just in your muscles, but in your nervous system. If you didn't: It's OK, just accept where you are and try again next time. This kind of bodily awareness is invaluable for ensuring you make well informed and beneficial movement decisions that allow you to maintain a healthy and injury-free practice that can help you to reprogram the body, the nervous system and the mind (brain) to help you live better.

22. The Myth: Boat Pose is a great core exercise that works your abs.

The Reality: Depends on how you do it.

You heard time and again the classic yoga pose, Paripurna Navasana (Boat Pose), described as the perfect ab toning move. But is it really? Well, that all depends on how it is taught. For example, some teachers will describe the asana as a pose that one performs while balancing on the "sitting bones" (ischial tuberosities). So, it is natural to give a cue like, "roll forward towards your sitting bones to find the point of balance." But if you follow this cue you will only use your abdominal muscles to stabilize your torso (or your back extensors, depending on the shape of your lumbar spine and the distance between your back and the floor and the relative length at which your muscles most like to work). Rolling forward also shifts most of the work into your psoas (hip flexor) and iliacus (hip flexor). Once you're there, if you are attempting to "open your chest" and you don't have the awareness or articulation to extend your thoracic spine versus your lumbar, you may be placing your rectus abdominus into an elongated shape.

Since muscles don't like working on very long or very short lengths (for most of us, at least, unless we have been practicing otherwise) this actually hinders that muscle's ability to do work. One could make an argument about the abdominals working eccentrically in this way, but still the psoas is doing more work.

This photo of Kim doing Boat Pose captures what we're talking about. There is no denying the abs will work to keep her stabilized. But the majority of the work is in her hip flexors and not her abdominals proper.

Now check out the second photo. She's in a more rounded shape than the previous one. Here she is rolled back, so that her weight is moving off her "sitting bones" and moving onto her sacrum. Her lower back is flexed, which makes her look "rounded." This shape actually puts the work in the rectus abdominus and internal and external obliques. She looks like she is just performing an extra hard "crunch;" the front of the ribs and the pubic bones are moving towards one another. Her abs are contracting and she'll "feel the burn" in them much more as she has to work harder to hold this position with the added weight of her legs attempting to pull her out of the rounded crunch shape. In this "boat" you are still using your hip flexors to lift the legs, but now the abdominals have work to harder. For some people it may be harder to extend through the thoracic spine, but this is truly the ab defining move.

One is not necessarily better than the other, but people who have "tight hips" (i.e. they have difficulty extending through their hip flexors) may get "tighter hips" by practicing the first boat as opposed to potentially strengthening the abs (concentrically) if they practice the second. So be aware of the cues given by less discriminating teachers.

23. The Myth: Don't Use Your Glutes in Bridge Pose (Setu Bandha Sarvangasana)! PART 1

The Reality: In order to lift your hips up in the air you must use your glutes.

We love treating group classes like an open forum for discussion of all things yoga, movement...and reality TV. Picture teachers in togas leading the class through Socratic dialogue. Recently, in one of these glorious moments of learning a student asked Mel, "When we're in bridge pose aren't we supposed to release the glutes?" Never had she heard of this cue, but others definitely had as evidenced by every other student in the class saying that they were also struggling to relax their butt muscles while holding the bridge shape.

No, people, you don't understand. Mel almost passed out. This had to be one of the most egregious cues in the history of movement anything. The student was asked what the purpose of this cue was and she said, "We are told to relax our glutes to release tension and strengthen the quads." Oh, it's just so bad.

> SOFTEN YOUR GLUTES

This fine tidbit is one of many tragic misinformation bombs that are dropped daily in yoga classes. Ok, so here's why not using your glutes while in bridge is a bad idea. You need to use your glutes to get your pelvis in the air in the first place. Ideally, the muscular work of this bridge is then distributed along the entire back line of your body. But the gluteals, hamstrings and calves are the dominant muscle groups used to maintain the shape and height of your bridge. What is being described here is a kinetic chain, a group of muscles working together. To interrupt an integral part of that chain, by releasing the buttock muscles, could be injurious especially with repetition. (Note: The push of the feet into the floor with a strong and well distributed force is also essential to the shape of this asana. But for the sake of time and keeping this book at a decent length we'll not go further into that.)

So, is it even possible to do bridge pose without the glutes?! Maybe...weird shit happens all the time, but it's doubtful.

You could probably eventually train your butt to relax when you've reached the top of your bridge. If you are successful you can expect your pelvis to drop, which means you won't get to experience the full length that your hip flexors and quads reach while achieving this hip extension. This stretch in the front of the body is a great reason to do bridge, especially if you spend a lot of time at a desk sitting (perpetual hip flexion). However, when the pelvis (i.e. physical support against gravity) drops in your new sad-bridge, those same quads and hip flexors could be overworked in a terrible compensation pattern resulting from desperate attempts to maintain length. Imagine an arch. This is the shape we are creating. But we are human and not stone. In order to create a nicely integrated shape it must be dynamic and the muscles of our backline contract to support the shape against gravitational and other compressive forces. Thus, in this asana: no gluteal support = inefficient compensation patterns. Also, the pelvis dropping a bit from its position could aggravate already present low back issues (chronic pain, stiffness, herniations, etc.).

When this was explained to the misled student mentioned above she asked, "Well, shouldn't we learn to do this pose supported by our bones?" We ask, "What moves your bones???"

24. The Myth: Don't use your glutes in Bridge Pose. PART 2

The Reality: A. we need to contract the glutes in order to do the pose well and B. many people today have glutes that don't work well from sitting all day!

[This is bonus content from Dana Santas: Yoga Teacher/Mobility Maker/Creator of Radius Yoga (radiusyoga.com)]

The glutes are essential muscles for sports performance and, arguably, all human "performance," which is why Glute Bridge is one of the primary postures in my athlete programs. One of my biggest pet peeves in general yoga instruction is teaching bridge pose as a backbend that shuts off glutes. My strength coach friends are saying, "What??!!" I hear you!

Below, I expand on my opinion of this all-too-common yoga cue and offer commentary from an athlete who practiced bridge pose with "relaxed glutes" and suffered stress fractures in their femur necks.

So what's wrong with teaching Bridge Pose in yoga as a backbend without glute activation? Too much focus is put on the upper body during bridging in yoga—either completely disregarding the core, pelvis and legs as the primary support in this pose or, worse yet, giving erroneous instructions to "soften" glutes. It's often taught as a prep pose for bigger backbends, so I understand the rationale, but I still disagree. In my experience, I've found yoga instruction for bigger backbends, like wheel, lacks emphasis on the pelvis and lower posterior chain…which, in turn, is likely why lower back strains are the most common reported reason for ER visits related to yoga (source: NEISS).

The injury risk of listening to a misinformed yoga instructor and "softening" your glutes in a pose like bridge is not just limited to your low back. Read on for some commentary from an athlete, aspiring strength coach and yoga enthusiast I mentored, who suffered stress fractures in the necks of her femurs:

> "I was in a yoga class where the teacher instructed the class to relax the glutes during bridge pose. I think the idea behind it was to use the "core" (which I guess only includes the stomach, lower back, and above) to lift up.
>
> The physical therapist thinks the stress fractures were caused by pain-induced muscle inhibition. I was likely putting too much wear and tear on my hips without having enough strength in the deeper supportive muscles that surround the pelvis. The pain caused the surrounding muscles to inhibit as a protective measure. Since the muscles were not firing properly, the bones were not being supported and therefore likely caused the stress fractures in the necks of the femurs.
>
> I don't believe my injury was caused by yoga, but the cue to not squeeze my butt in bridge probably didn't help me to avoid injury."

Yikes! This is precisely why I caution my pro athletes not to attend public yoga classes—even (sometimes, especially) the ones marketed to athletes—without vetting the instructor. Unbelievably, not every yoga certification program teaches biomechanics. In fact, Yoga Alliance's credential requirements enable anatomy hours to be solely focused on Chakras at the discretion of the "yoga school." Just saying…

25. The Myth: The more Chaturangas you do, the stronger your arms and shoulders will be.

The Reality: The more Chaturangas you do the more likely you are to injure your shoulders or create a musculoskeletal imbalance.

If you do a lot of power yoga or vinyasa flow classes then chances are that you're doing 20-50 Chaturangas per class. If you're a teacher then you've probably noticed that the majority of your students aren't doing them with integrity so they're likely making their postural issues worse and creating a musculoskeletal imbalance in the glenohumeral (shoulder) joint - hypertonic (overdeveloped, relatively) triceps, anterior deltoid, pectoralis minor and pectoralis major, hypotonic (underdeveloped, relatively) biceps, rear deltoids and lats. This brings us back to an earlier point that yoga doesn't strengthen pulling muscles.

The shoulder joint is one of the most complicated and unstable joints in the human body. The shallow structure of the curved edge of the glenoid fossa (scapula) in which the head of the humerus sits makes this joint far less stable than the hip joint. As bipeds, this allows us better range of motion and more movement options in our upper bodies. But this mobility translates to instability and the potential risk for injury when trying to repeatedly bear weight on a not-meant-for-weight-bearing part of the body.

The front of the shoulder joint is most at risk since it is the least structurally sound (less bony protection). Let's suppose you can properly maintain core strength/spinal alignment. But now, you must stabilize the shoulder complex, especially as you bend through the elbows. This means that your shoulder blades don't peel off your ribs, a movement known as "winging." Scapular stabilization is related to strength and the proper function (timing) of your rotator cuff muscles, lats, anterior serratus, pecs, trapezius, etc. The size and shape of your scapulae and the heads of your humerus will influence how well you can control the shoulder blades in Chaturanga.

Maintaining a full Plank with scapular stability is a healthier place to start when trying to build up to Chaturangas. Then move on to practicing pushups with the arms and hands wide away from the body. This is a less strenuous position for the shoulder joint. If the second you start lowering to the floor (bending your elbows) your shoulder blades start winging off your rib cage then you should assess, with the help of a movement professional, what you need to do to progress in a healthy way. While in yoga class, you should evaluate how ready you are for advanced vinyasa flows which include many Chaturangas as you transition into other poses. (Note to ego: Just drop to your knees when making these transitions until you're ready. Or don't and end up with scapular dysfunction.)

Not all Yoga moves are appropriate for all bodies. This may be disappointing, but it's true. One of the biggest lies/misconceptions about a yoga practice is that it has to look a certain way or that your physical self must somehow conform to a specific style of performance. Not true. At All. If you know that doing Chaturangas, or any other asana, hurts then stop. You don't have to include it. If you want it then go about pursuing your goals intelligently. Don't believe the hype about practicing everyday to get stronger. Practicing the same pattern over and over will only (maybe!) make you stronger in that pattern. So, whatever you can't correct you could be making worse by insistent repetition leading to overuse injuries.

26. The Myth: Your transition from Downward Dog (Adho Muka Svanasana) to Plank should be seamless. If you have to adjust your feet, you're doing it wrong.

The Reality: We all have different body proportions. It's fine to adjust your feet if you feel like you need to.

Ever have that frustrating moment when you move from Downward Dog (Adho Mukha Svanasana) into Plank Pose and you find yourself having to readjust your feet or hands (i.e. your Plank is too "short" or too "long")? Have you heard your teacher tell you that your hand and foot positions should be exactly the same in Downward Dog and Plank? We have! Articles online[1] and videos try to demonstrate this technique as a way to make your practice "fool proof." But the truth is that this direction will NOT work for EVERY BODY. Don't you love being set up for failure?

Let's talk about body proportion. It's pretty simple: If someone has really short arms in comparison to the length of their torso and legs then there will definitely be shifting of hand and feet positions when transitioning from dog to plank. Vice versa, if someone's legs are really short in comparison to the above proportions that will also entail shifting. The usual direction to, "Get on all fours. Keep your hands directly under your shoulders and your knees a bit behind your pelvis, now lift the pelvis into the air," does not take into account the individual differences between torso and limb lengths when then transitioning into plank. Therefore, if you're in class and you hear these kind of guidelines be aware that they may not apply to you and don't think there's something wrong with you or your practice.

You may just have to shift to get the "correct" positioning from D-dog to Plank, IF you want an elongated spine. If you are actually trying to work your abdominals in a different way then moving into it with the pelvis tucked under a bit can be useful (be aware if you are also rounding the shoulders and thoracic spine, if that's not what you intend to do). Think of it as an upside down boat pose. Or if you're really opposed to the idea of having to shift hands and feet every time (which we kind of don't get. What's wrong with moving around anyways? Yoga IS a MOVEMENT practice.) then just bend your knees. Voila! If you happen to move into a short plank, but want the extended version or you're not getting the spinal extension you want in d-dog then bend your knees. This is the direction they give for "tight" or "short" hamstrings anyways right? There is a relationship between the back of the legs and the spine. You can negotiate this relationship so that you find a functional compromise (not struggle and force something that causes injury or frustration) and apply that same technique to this particular transition. And yes, you can do a Plank with bent knees. Try it…how are your abs feeling now? How does this affect your experience?

Play with this idea the next time you do yoga. Can you adopt certain modifications that make your practice adapt to your body, reducing stress, frustration and allowing for exploration (isn't that why we do yoga anyway)? Or are you trying to force your body to adapt to a practice with guidelines constructed out of theories that don't always apply to everyone the same way? Put your tapas[2] where your mouth is (yeah, we said it) and create a yoga practice that really is individualized for you instead of just saying that's what you do. Teachers, same goes for you. Allow students to embody each asana in a personal way. Don't be afraid to move beyond clichés and create classes that allow each unique student to gain the idiosyncratic benefits of a personalized practice.

If you'd like to learn more about body proportions and yoga, watch this short video on the SMARTer Bodies Blog.[3]

27. The Myth: Shoulderstand (Salamba Sarvangasana) and Headstand (Sirsasana) are the king and queen of yoga poses. It's ideal to do them in every practice and aim to do each one for 10 minutes.

The Reality: These are not the king and queen of poses for the general, modern western population. The general population's bodies aren't prepared to bear all of their body weight on the small bones of their neck.

Generic promises of health and vitality are associated with these poses. It's also been said that Sirsasana heats the body while Sarvangasana cools it and we need both to achieve balance. We've read in recent mainstream publications that Shoulderstand can balance hormones, cure constipation and

Myths About Poses

the common cold, strengthen the heart and respiratory system, decrease varicose veins, stimulate the root chakra, aid in sleep and reduce wrinkles. We've also read that Headstand can improve digestion, relieve depression, increase blood flow to the eyes, improve brain function and nourish the face (Ariana's favorite). There are many more claims that these poses cure "most common ailments". AYFKM? To say the least, these supposed benefits are unsupported by medical literature.

We believe these poses are inappropriate for most group yoga classes. In most cases, students' necks aren't prepared to

support the weight of their bodies in these inverted positions. Especially because the general population tends to suffer from modern musculoskeletal "dysfunction" such as forward head posture and limited range of motion in the shoulders. We only teach these poses to our private clients if their joints are ready for it and, of course, if they want to do them.

Sadly, there are many who feel that a yoga practice is incomplete without including both of these poses. We rarely do these postures ourselves anymore. See how Mel's body (in the pic here) is not in a perfectly vertical line? That's a conscious decision. Mel feels an uncomfortable and unhealthy amount of pressure on her upperback, neck and skull when doing shoulderstand without props, like a blanket under her shoulders. So trying to go any farther than this could be potentially dangerous. Yay! Ego loses. Mel's spine wins.

We have seen many students who feel that if they cannot do Shoulderstand without props, their practice is inauthentic. The truth is Shoulderstand puts the neck at risk. Our cervical spines should naturally have a lordotic (forward) curvature to be functional. Bending the neck at this angle is not only

uncomfortable, but staying in this position for long periods of time can decrease this natural, functional curvature. Some Iyengar texts and teachers recommend headstand and shoulderstand for a minimum of 10 minutes a day...we advise against this. It is often excessive flexion that can cause bulging disks that hit nerves. When assessing these potential risks, it is probably the case that they outweigh the purported benefits.

Like shoulderstand, headstand presents an unnatural position for our bodies. When examining the structure of our bones, it is clear that the pelvis and the feet are designed to bear the weight of our bodies. Our skulls? Not so much. The tiny bones of our neck compared to the large bones in our lumbar spine are also further evidence that we should probably not be in this position for very long. Again, we have to wonder about the risk vs. benefit factor here.

28. The Myth: Lotus Pose (Padmasana) is the ideal meditation seat.

The Reality: Our western (chair sitting) bodies can rarely tolerate that position.

In many yoga traditions Lotus Pose is referred to as an ideal position for seated meditation. We've heard claims that being able to place the heel to the abdomen creates an "energetic seal," or stimulates an energetic point for a better meditation practice. However, Lotus requires extreme external rotation at the hip joint which most Western bodies are not prepared for and some bodies may not be able to do at all from a structural point of view (the angle of the neck of the femur is an influence here). If your hips do not have that range of motion and you keep trying to force your foot onto your thigh something will give and it's, unfortunately, usually the knee. If the thigh cannot externally rotate relative to the pelvis and you keep forcing the position then the tibia might rotate more than the femur causing torsion and a meniscus tear or ligament sprain. This is one of the more common yoga-related injuries.

The ideal meditation posture is one in which you have a balance of ease and effort, and can breathe comfortably while maintaining the position for the duration of your meditation. It is important to feel comfortable so that you don't strain your

joints (and to foster a positive meditation practice that you'll actually want to come back to instead of avoid). It's more of a challenge to sustain a meditation practice if you're dealing with the distraction of pain or discomfort. We encourage clients to recognize that there is discomfort and find another way to sit rather than push through or ignore the pain.
If you spend a lot of time meditating then it's a good idea to switch up your meditation seat so that you avoid a repetitive strain injury.

FIN

that's all there is. there isn't any more.
just kidding.
there's a second volume coming out with
more technical information!

About the Authors

Kim-Lien Kendall is the co-founder of SMARTer Bodies and co-creator of SMARTer Yoga™. Her experience in gymnastics, sports, martial arts, dance and yoga combined with years of study in anatomy, kinesiology, biochemistry, bio-mechanics, corrective exercise and somatic movement education have equipped her with the knowledge and skill set to work with a wide range of clientele. Kim has been working professionally with bodies since 2005. She is currently the C.E.O. of SMARTer Bodies, the co-creator of SMARTer Yoga™, as well as a yoga instructor and personal trainer at Golf & Body NYC and has served as an adjunct professor for the H+ Dance Conservatory. She has a BS in Biochemistry from Florida State University (2005), is certified by Yoga Union (2006), is a NASM personal trainer, has completed training and an ongoing education at the Breathing Project, is certified by Redcord Active and has been certified as a MET Master Facilitator.

About the Authors

Melissa Gutierrez is the co-founder of SMARTer Bodies and co-creator of SMARTer Yoga™. Her practices as a yoga teacher, energy worker and somatic educator have led to many therapeutic discoveries. She is considered an expert in creating movement patterns that help clients release physically, emotionally and mentally to create extraordinary results. To work with Mel is to integrate your body and mental state so that you can move in space in ways you may never have imagined possible. Melissa has a B.A. in Psychology/Religious Studies from Smith College (2003), has certificates from Karuna center for yoga, the Breathing Project, is a level 2 Reiki practitioner, is Redcord Active certified and has ongoing education studying different forms of somatic movement.

About the Authors

Ariana Rabinovitch is a Yoga Teacher//Human Movement Science Geek and the host of the Yoga & Beyond Podcast where she interviews yoga, movement and wellness experts. She also created the Foundations of Movement class, a mindful practice that focuses on mastering the basics of good movement. Her goal is to help people move better so they can live better. With a straight-forward approach that combines yoga and movement, she helps students restore mobility, prevent injury and boost energy. She holds a number of yoga and movement certifications including YogaWorks, Anatomy Studies for Yoga Teachers, Yoga Tune Up®, NKT®, FRCms, FMS and more.

Notes & Sources

It's important to us to remain humble and acknowledge the sources of wisdom that have helped us to refine our teachings and practices. It is a blessing to live in a time where information is freely available. For us, our integrity as teachers is made, in part, by naming and sharing these sources.

Myth 1: Yoga as we know it in the Modern West isn't real yoga, it's not pure.

1. Iyengar, B.K.S. (1966). Light on Yoga. New York, NY: Schocken Books Inc.

2. Iyengar, B.K.S. (1996). Light on the Yoga Sutras of Patanjali. Hammersmith, London: HarperCollinsPublishers.

3. Desikachar, T.K.V. (1995). The Heart of Yoga. Rochester, VT: Inner Traditions International.

4. Mark Singleton, "The Roots of Yoga: Ancient + Modern," available at http://www.yogajournal.com/article/philosophy/yoga-s-greater-truth/

5. Schroeder, M. (Producer), & Schmidt-Garre, J. (Director). (2012). Breath of the gods. [Motion Picture]. United States of America: PARS Media.

Notes & Sources

Myth 2: Yoga builds lean, slim muscle.

1. Contreras, B. "Long, Lean Muscles: Oh, the Irony," available at http://bretcontreras.com/long-lean-muscles-oh-irony/

2. John Leyva, "How Do Muscles Grow? The Science of Muscle Growth," available at http://www.builtlean.com/2013/09/17/muscles-grow/

3. Velloso, C.P. (2008). Regulation of muscle mass by growth hormone and IGF-I. British Journal of Pharmacology, 154(3), 557–568.

4. Available at http://www.ncbi.nlm.nih.gov/pmc/articles/PMC2439518/

Myth 5: Yoga is the only kind of movement you need.

1. Retrieved on April 3, 2013 from MayoClinic: http://newsnetwork.mayoclinic.org/discussion/exercise-best-medicine-to-prevent-alzheimers/

2. Retrieved on April 3, 2013 from Wikipedia: https://en.wikipedia.org/wiki/Shoshin

Myth 9: You can't get hurt practicing yoga.

1. VLAHOS, J. (2011, April 14). Is sitting a lethal activity? The New York Times. Retrieved from: http://www.nytimes.com/2011/04/17/magazine/mag-17sitting-t.html?_r=0

Notes & Sources

2. Broad, W.J. (2012, January 5). How yoga can wreck your body. The New York Times. Retrieved from: http://www.nytimes.com/2012/01/08/magazine/how-yoga-can-wreck-your-body.html?_r=0

Myth 10: Hot yoga detoxifies the body and helps you burn more calories.

1. Cancer research is a vast and ever-growing field. If you are interesting in metabolic studies behind certain cancers start here: Fasting Cycles Retard Growth of Tumors and Sensitize a Range of Cancer Cell Types to Chemotherapy, from the Journal of Science Translational Medicine, Vol. 4, Issue 124, pp. 124 - 127. http://stm.sciencemag.org/content/4/124/124ra27

2. McGinnis, M. "Sweat is 99% Water, 1% Natural Stuff and 0% Toxins," available at http://footloveyoga.com/2015/09/07/sweat-is-99-water-1-natural-stuff-and-0-toxins/

Myth 11: Always be gentle with your body. Don't push. Be super careful with yourself. Stress is bad for you.

1. McGonigal, K. (2013, June). How to Make Stress Your Friend [Video File]. Retrieved from

2. http://www.ted.com/talks/kelly_mcgonigal_how_to_make_stress_your_friend?language=en

3. We first wrote this blog post in January 2013. At the time Yoga Journal had an issue with an article

advising older practitioners be careful and use props. We read it, but didn't bother to keep track of what the issue number was. We never thought we'd need it for a future book.

4. Retrieved on August 30, 2013 from CDC: http://www.cdc.gov/homeandrecreationalsafety/falls/adultfalls.html

5. Retrieved on August 30, 2013 from Healing Back Pain: http://www.healingbackpain.com/books.html

6. O'Sullivan, P. (2015, September). Back Pain - Separating Fact from Fiction [Video File].

7. Retrieved from https://www.youtube.com/watch?v=dlSQLUE4brQ

8. http://www.smarterbodies.com/yoga/let-your-organs-support-you/

13. The Myth: You should always do yoga poses on the right side before the left.

1. Info about SMARTer Yoga™: http://www.smarterbodies.com/smarter-yoga/

2. Info about Foundations of Movement: http://www.arianayoga.com/foundations-of-good-movement/

Myth 14: Squeeze your shoulder blades together and press your shoulders down your back all the time.

1. Osar, E. (2014). Corrective Exercise Solutions to Common Hip and Shoulder Dysfunction. Apple Tree Cottage, Inlands Road, Nutbourne, Chichester: Lotus Publishing.

Myth 18: In order to use Mula Bandha in a yoga pose, you need to contract the muscles of the anus and urethra like you're holding back urine.

1. Iyengar, B.K.S. (1966). Light on Yoga. New York, NY: Schocken Books Inc.

2. Franklin, E. (2003). Pelvic Power: Mind/Body Exercises for Strength, Flexibility, Posture, and Balance. Hightstown, NJ: Princeton Book Publishers.

3. http://www.smarterbodies.com/yoga/the-low-down-on-pelvic-floor-exercises/

Myth 19: Twists wring out the organs and detoxify the body.

1. Retrieved on July 4, 2012 from Wikipedia: https://en.wikipedia.org/wiki/Peritoneum

2. http://www.smarterbodies.com/health/your-breathing-is-related-to-your-indigestion/

3. http://www.coneyisland.com/programs/mermaid-parade

Myth 21: Turning your head makes your Twist bigger!

1. Like that nifty little box with the degrees of cervical rotation? So do we! Ariana made it, because she's a badass like that. It's data collected from a combination of sources: Diane Lee, Evan Osar, Wikipedia and Dr. Joseph E. Muscolino.

Myth 26: Your transition from Downward Dog (Adho Muka Svanasana) to Plank should be seamless. If you have to adjust your feet, you're doing it wrong.

1. Retrieved on October 22, 2012 from About Health: http://yoga.about.com/od/yogaposes/a/downdog.htm

2. Retrieved on October 22, 2012 from Wikipedia: https://en.wikipedia.org/wiki/Tapas_%28Sanskrit%29

3. Retrieved on October 8, 2015 from SMARTer Bodies Blog: http://www.smarterbodies.com/yoga/body-shapes/

Glossary

Many of the definitions have been pulled from different sources, but are also an amalgamated understanding from years of continuing education. We wanted to share important sources that provide definitions we trust and so that you can further pursue reading if you would like. Remember, whatever you read, especially internet articles, should be done so with a critical eye and a willingness to independently fact check.

Biel, A. (2015). Trail Guide to Movement: Building the Body in Motion (1st ed). Boulder, CO: Books of Discovery.

Bowman, K. (2014). Move Your DNA: Restore Your Health Through Natural Movement. Carlsborg, WA: Propriometrics Press.

Cook, G., Burton, L., Kiesel, K., Rose, G., Bryan, F. (2010). Movement: Functional Movement Systems: Screening, Assessment, Corrective Strategies. Aptos, CA: On Target Publications.APTOS. CA

Gershon, M.D. (1998). The Second Brain: A Groundbreaking New Understanding of Nervous Disorder of the Stomach and Intestine. New York, NY: HarperCollins Publishers.

Hargrove, T. (2014). A Guide to Better Movement: The Science and Practice of Moving With More Skill And Less Pain. Seattle, WA: Better Movement.

Juhan, D. (1987). Job's Body: A Handbook for Bodywork. Barrytown, NY: Station Hill Press.

Kaminoff, L., Matthews, A., (2012). Yoga Anatomy (2nd ed.). Champaign, IL: Human Kinetics.

Martini, F. H., Bartholomew, E. F. (2000). Essentials of Anatomy and Physiology (2nd ed.). Princeton, NJ: Prentice-Hall, Inc.

Myers, T. (2009). Anatomy Trains: Myofascial Meridians for Manual and Movement Therapists (2nd. ed). New York, NY: Churchill Livingstone.

Osar, E. (2014). Corrective Exercise Solutions to Common Hip and Shoulder Dysfunction. Apple Tree Cottage, Inlands Road, Nutbourne, Chichester: Lotus Publishing.

Schultz, R. L., Feitis, R. (1996). The Endless Web: Fascial Anatomy and Physical Reality. Berkeley, CA: North Atlantic Books.

Glossary

Want to brush up on your technical vocabulary? We wanted to make it easy for you to do so. Continually rechecking your information is the way to make sure what you communicate is solid and consistent. So go ahead! Grab some sake, sit back and prepare to impress your students, friends and colleagues.

ASANA - Sanskrit, which means, "seat." Refers to the positions in the physical practice of yoga.

CENTRATION - Refers to positioning a joint so that there is an equal amount of negative space within it.

CONTRALATERAL - Of relating to the opposite side.

CENTRAL NERVOUS SYSTEM (CNS) - Made up of the brain and the spinal cord, refers to their activity in processing information and controlling how other systems in the body respond. Includes the Somatic nervous system and the Autonomic nervous system.

ELASTICITY - The capacity of tissues (in the body) to recoil or rebound to an original length or shape after being stretched (or deformed).

ENTERIC NERVOUS SYSTEM - The network of nerves embedded in the lining of the gastrointestinal system, beginning in the esophagus and extending down to the anus. This nerve system can function even when its connection to the spinal cord has been removed making it "independent" and unique. Increasingly acknowledged as another part of the CNS the system is made up of two nerve plexus: Meissner's and Auerbach's.

EXTEROCEPTION - The process of being sensitive to and interpreting stimuli outside of the physical body (i.e. temperature, pressure, vibrations, etc.).

INTEROCEPTION - The process of sensing physiological stimuli from within the body (i.e. neurological information from organs).

HOMEOSTASIS - The maintenance of a relatively constant internal environment through adjustments in physiological systems (i.e. blood pressure, temperature, metabolism)

NEUROPLASTICITY - The brain's ability to change.

PERITONEUM - The sack of connective tissue that contains most of the internal organs.

PARASYMPATHETIC NERVOUS SYSTEM - One part of the 2-part Autonomic nervous system, generally responsible for activities that conserve energy and lower the metabolic rate. Commonly referred to as the "rest and digest" part of the nervous system. Clinically referred to as the craniosacral division.

PERIPHERAL NERVOUS SYSTEM (PNS) - Refers to the CNS interacting with other sense organs and systems. Includes all neural tissue outside of the CNS (i.e. nerves, ganglia).

PROPRIOCEPTION - The ability to sense where one's body is in space via specific nerves in muscles and fascia.

SAID PRINCIPLE - Specific Adaptation to Imposed Demands. A training principle that asserts that the brain and body will adapt to particular stresses.

SCAPULOHUMERAL RHYTHM - Describes the coordinated movement of the scapula on the rib cage and humerus (in the glenohumeral joint) to successfully abduct/adduct, internally/externally rotate, flex/extend the arm and explore full range of motion. There are specific and defined degrees of movement between these 2 bones depending on the arm's position/angle to the body.

STRENGTHEN - (In the context of muscles) To train muscle tissue to function under a load/weight at a certain length. Not really different from "stretching." See stretching.

STRETCH(ING) - (In the context of muscles) Elongate muscle tissue. This is also considered "strengthening," particularly if you are training your muscles to function at a length they are not used to while supporting a load/weight.

SYMPATHETIC NERVOUS SYSTEM - One part of the 2-part Autonomic nervous system, primarily concerned with the elevation of metabolic rate and increased alertness. Commonly referred to as the "fight or flight part of the nervous system.

Sanskrit Index

ADHO MUKA SVANASANA - Downward Dog, Myth 26

CHATURANGA DANDASANA - Four-limbed Staff Pose, Myth 4, Myth 5

PADMASANA - Lotus Pose, Myth 28

PARIPURNA NAVASANA - Boat Pose, Myth 22

PARIVRTTA PARSVAKONASANA - Revolved Side Angle Pose, Myth 4

SETU BANDHA SARVANGASANA - Bridge Pose, Myth 23, Myth 24

TAPAS - The "fire" and "heat" of your practice, the discipline/intention you bring to it, Myth 26

TRIKONASANA - Triangle Pose, Myth 4

UJJAYI - The Sanskrit translation is very complicated here, so for our purposes, "Whispered Breath," Myth 12

UTKATASANA - Awkward Chair Pose, Myth 4

SALAMBA SARVANGASANA - Shoulderstand, Myth 27

SIRSASANA - Headstand, Myth 27

Index

A

adjustments 42-43, 45

Ahimsa 3

Ashtanga 13

B

back pain 31, 32

Bhagavad Gita 7

Bikram 13

Boat Pose 22, 59, 60, 70

Bridge Pose 61, 62, 64, 65

C

Chair Pose 15, 22

Chaturanga 15, 19, 22, 66-68

Cobra Pose 45

connective tissue 12, 50, 54, 57

D

Desikachar 9

detoxification 27

Downward Dog 22, 41, 68, 69

E

enteric nervous system 38, 53

F

facet joints 57

flexibility 11, 22, 25, 57, 59

G

Genetics 10-12

glutes 61, 62, 64, 65

gravity 11, 22, 23, 30, 41, 42, 54, 63

H

Handstand 41

Headstand 71-73

Hinduism 7

hip extension 22, 23, 63

Hot yoga 27-29, 47

I

IGF-1 12

Iyengar 9, 49, 73

J

joint centration 22

K

Krishnamacharya 4, 8, 9

L

Lotus Pose 74

M

meditation 4, 13, 37, 55, 74, 75

Mula Bandha 49

N

Neuroplasticity 17

Neuroscience 3, 39

O

organs 2, 33, 34, 50-57

P

Patanjali 7, 8

Pattabhi Jois 9, 13

pelvic floor 49, 50

personal trainer 42, 44

Plank 22, 67, 68, 69, 70

pranayama 8, 13, 37

props 30, 73

psoas 60

push ups 19

R

rectus abdominus 60, 61

rotator cuff 42, 67

S

SAID principle 24

Savasana 37

scapulae 40, 67

scapulohumeral rhythm 41

shoulder blades 39, 40, 41

shoulder joint 77, 68

Shoulderstand 71, 73

strength training 46

stress 13, 14, 18, 26-27, 29, 34 - 35

Sutras 7

T

tapas 71

toxins 27, 28, 36, 51, 52

Triangle Pose 15

twists 2, 38, 50, 51, 53

U

Ujjayi 36, 37

W

workout 11, 19, 20, 21, 29

Y

Yamas 3

Yoga Alliance 44, 66

Yoga Journal 30

Z

Zen Buddhism 18

Made in the USA
Lexington, KY
26 April 2017